TM 5-805-7
Welding
Design, Procedures and Inspection
May 1985

This manual contains criteria and basic data for welded construction design, construction methods, and inspection procedures for Army construction. This manual covers only the following welding processes and materials commonly used for field construction projects: shielded metal-arc, gas metal-arc, gas tungsten-arc , flux-cored arc, submerged arc, exothermic, and arc stud welding processes. Discussions of physics, chemistry, and metallurgy are limited to areas helpful in selecting welding processes, materials, and inspection procedures for the applications listed.

Should you have suggestions or feedback on ways to improve this book please send email to Books@OcotilloPress.com

Edited 2021 Ocotillo Press
ISBN 978-1-954285-57-6

Ocotillo Press
Houston, TX 77017
Books@OcotilloPress.com

TM 5-805-7

TECHNICAL MANUAL

WELDING

DESIGN, PROCEDURES AND INSPECTION

HEADQUARTERS, DEPARTMENT OF THE ARMY

20 MAY 1985

REPRODUCTION AUTHORIZATION/RESTRICTIONS

Technical Manual
No. 5-805-7

HEADQUARTERS
Department of the Army
Washington, DC, *20 May 1985*

WELDING: DESIGN, PROCEDURES AND INSPECTION

---

*This manual supersedes TM 5-805-7, dated 15 March 1968, including all changes.

LIST OF FIGURES

LIST OF TABLES

CHAPTER 1

INTRODUCTION

1-1. Purpose and scope

This manual contains criteria and basic data for welded construction design, construction methods, and inspection procedures for Army construction. This manual covers only the following welding processes and materials commonly used for field construction projects: shielded metal-arc, gas metal-arc, gas tungsten-arc , flux-cored arc, submerged arc, exothermic, and arc stud welding processes. Discussions of physics, chemistry, and metallurgy are limited to areas helpful in selecting welding processes, materials, and inspection procedures for the applications listed in paragraph 1-3. For supplemental information, see the American Welding Society (AWS) *Welding Handbook* (available in five sections) and TM 9-237. Appendix A lists other works, codes, and specifications which are referenced in this manual; designers should note that there are differences among the documents' requirements. Therefore, when this material is used, the editions which apply to a given design must be specified.

1-2. Welding applications

This manual discusses the following materials.

a. Steel.

(1) Structural carbon steel welded to structural carbon steel.

(2) Structural carbon steel welded to high-strength, low-alloy steel.

(3) High-strength, low-alloy steel welded to high-strength, low-alloy steel.

(4) Carbon or high-strength, low-alloy steels for all types of piping systems.

(5) Concrete reinforcing steel.

(6) Rails.

(7) Steel castings, either carbon or high-strength, low-alloy.

b. Stainless steels.

(1) Cryogenic vessels and piping materials used for storage and transport of extremely low-temperature liquids.

(2) Vacuum chambers.

(3) All other uses.

c. Nickel steels and nickel alloys for cryogenic vessels and piping systems.

d. Aluminum alloys for cryogenic vessels, piping systems, and other uses.

e. Carbon and high-strength, low-alloy steels welded to stainless steels. An example of this use is when steel supports or stiffeners are attached to stainless steel vessels.

CHAPTER 2

DESIGN AND INSPECTION RESPONSIBILITIES

2-1. Designer responsibilities

a. The designer must specify the base metal for the structure, according to design and service requirements and provide essential metallurgical and design information in the specifications. Welding process and filler metals are selected by the fabricator or, in some cases, specified by the design office to fit the material requirements; these items should be included in the specifications and indicated on the drawings. The joint designs must be shown on the drawings by a standard welding symbol or by detailed drawings of the weld joints.

b. The designer must determine the welding requirements, and must develop or select the appropriate welding sections of the contract for each project. These decisions are based on instructions from the using agency. The designer must develop contract specifications that ensure the contractor knows the welding quality that must be maintained. The designer uses the following criteria to determine the required degree of control over welding quality.

(1) Strict control over welding procedures and operations is required in five cases (listed in order of increasing importance):

(a) Distress in one member could cause at least partial collapse or failure with some hazard to life and property; application of the design load may approach 10,000 cycles over many years.

(b) Some of the welds required for structural integrity are highly stressed; application of the design load may exceed 10,000 cycles over many years.

(c) Empirical design requirements compensate for overloads, abuse, mishandling, "acts of God," and similar hazards; application of the design load may be on the order of 100,000 cycles.

(d) Failure of welds or components could be catastrophic, as in structures such as bridges or high-pressure gas piping systems ; fatigue of materials must be carefully considered or application of design load is on the order of 2 million cycles.

(e) Applications require the highest quality of material and workmanship throughout, such as for nuclear, space, and ballistic applications and for systems subjected to hazardous chemicals, or extreme pressures or temperatures.

(2) Less control over welding procedures and operations is needed where:

(a) Stress levels are low.

(b) Welds are subjected only occasionally to design loads.

(c) The structure is composed of multiple components, and distress in one member will cause inconvenience rather than collapse or catastrophic failure.

c. The designer must establish the inspection procedures needed to determine the weld quality. The designer must be familiar with the destructive and nondestructive methods of evaluating weld quality and must know their capabilities and limitations. Procedures to qualify inspectors must be specified.

d. The designer must establish the acceptance requirements for the welded joints, and must identify the applicable military standards, specifications, and codes for meeting these requirements. When standards, codes, and other specifications are cited, the contract specification must list the paragraphs or parts of the publications which are applicable or excluded. The designer must use only the most recent codes and specifications.

e. The designer must indicate on the plans or specifications the extent of inspection and testing required for the various applications and conditions. Although the inspection and testing needed depend primarily on the design requirements, the following general guidelines should be considered.

(1) Apply value engineering — in short, do not specify unnecessary testing.

(2) Follow design criteria and codes that specify the extent of inspection and testing required relative to working stresses, joint efficiencies, or conditions of use.

(3) Inspect visually in noncritical applications or conditions; very little other testing should be required.

(4) Identify the critical joints and welds and choose those to be tested. The criticality of each weld should determine the extent of nondestructive and destructive tests; these tests supplement the quality control provided by qualified procedures, qualified welders and operators, and visual inspection. The weld can be critical because of high stresses, impact, vibration, temperature, safety, insurance against operational failure, hard-to-weld material, or a combination of these factors. In a multistory office or warehouse building with structural

steel framing, for example, testing would be done mainly at the highly stressed joints. In a critical piping system, however, either all joints would be nondestructively tested or a uniformly applied random test procedure would be used.

(5) Determine the extent of random testing in piping, tanks, and other elements that have uniform joints and design levels. This number can be expressed as a percentage of all welds in the system, coupled with a finite test increment. However, the extent of random testing in large steel structures with a variety of welds and widely varying design stresses should not be expressed this way. The designer is responsible for specifying the appropriate tests for critical and noncritical welds. To insure clarity in bidding and inspection documents, the location, numbers, and minimum increment lengths of the random tests should be clearly outlined.

f. The designer must indicate in the specification what to do when welds fail to meet acceptance requirements.

g. The designer must design the weld so that the operator can reach the weld joint easily. If the joint is located so that the welder cannot observe the welding operation easily or position the welding gun or electrode properly, a poor weld may result. In such cases, it may be hard or impossible to repair any weld defects.

(1) The dimensions and shape of the joint surfaces should allow the weld metal to penetrate the joint fully. If pieces of different thicknesses are to be joined, the edge of the thicker piece should be tapered to the thickness of the thinner piece. The tapered transitions must conform to the requirements of the following publications, as applicable: AWS D1.1; the American Society of Mechanical Engineers (ASME) Boiler and Pressure Vessel Code, Section III or Section VIII; or the American National Standards Institute (ANSI) Standard B 31.1.

(2) Good joint design practices for vessels are shown in section VIII of the ASME Boiler and Pressure Vessel Code; for piping in appendix D of ANSI B31.1; and for structural work in the American Institute of Steel Construction's (AISC) *Manual of Steel Construction* and AWS Dl.1.

(3) In some welding operations, some type of weld joint backing is used to support the molten weld metal and prevent excessive penetration. Backing strips, when used, must be of material similar to the base metals which are penetrated by the weld metal. Nonconsumable" 'backing rings in piping systems should not be permitted unless absolutely necessary. Instead, penetration can be controlled by altering the joint design (increasing the root face or decreasing the root opening) or by using consumable insert rings.

(4) If the joint is welded from both sides, the reverse side of the root pass (the side opposite that on which the weld was deposited) should be chipped, ground, or gouged out to sound metal before any welding is done from the second side. This operation will prevent lack of fusion at the root of the joint. The reverse side of single "V" weld joints may also be ground out and rewelded to improve the contour. Complete penetration groove welds must be welded from both sides unless a proper backup plate is used.

h. The designer must decide which welds are to be peened and which are not and indicate them on the drawings. Peening is the mechanical working of metals by hammer blows. This technique is useful for reducing distortion and residual stresses caused by shrinkage of the weld metal as it cools. However, the technique can be harmful if extreme care is not used. Since it can cause cracking, overlapping, or other defects, peening is not permitted on surface passes of the weld joints. Intermediate passes may be peened only with the contracting officer's permission. Peening of stainless steel welds is not permitted because it causes hardening of the weld metal. Care should be taken to prevent peening when slag is removed from the surface pass with chipping hammers.

i. The designer must determine if the shape of the weld surface and its height above the base metal (reinforcement) are important and indicate the shape on the drawings. An abrupt change in contour between the weld surface and the base metal may result in stress concentrations high enough to cause failure under service loadings. Therefore, the weld surface should blend smoothly into the surface of the base metal. If necessary, the edges of the weld should be ground to achieve a smooth blend of surfaces.

(1) Undercut at the edge of the weld can be repaired by grinding if the depth of undercut does not exceed 1/1 6 inch. If undercut is deeper than 1/16 inch, it should be repaired by adding weld metal to this area and then grinding the surface to a smooth, even contour.

(2) Grinding also should be used to remove overlap at the weld edges and any abrupt ridges or valleys in the weld surface.

(3) The maximum amount of weld reinforcement should be between 1/32 and 1/8 inch.

2-2. Contractor responsibilities

a. The contractor must develop a qualified welding procedure, provide qualified welders and welding operators, and produce satisfactory weldment.

(1) The construction drawings and specifications ordinarily indicate the location of the weld joints and the type of joint required, but the contractor must handle the details of producing the weld — for example, the equipment used, number of passes, choice of electrode, and welding process. Therefore, the contractor must understand the objective of the plans and, if necessary, seek guidance from the contracting officer and the welding engineer or metallurgist assigned to the project. Those concerned should meet to discuss the status of the welding program as work progresses.

(2) All welding procedures used for any of the applications covered by this manual and all welders and welding operators assigned to these construction operations must be qualified before production welding is begun. The contractor must conduct all qualification, testing and maintain records showing the testing procedures used and the results of these tests. These records must always be available to the inspector and the contracting officer or his representative.

b. The contractor must make sure the welding equiprnent is serviced and maintained properly to produce the required current output, voltage control, and filler wire feed rate for automatic and semi-automatic processes. Storage and handling of flux and coated electrodes must also be done properly.

(1) Flux must be kept free of dirt, mill scale, and other foreign material. Flux fused during previous welding operations should not be reused. If there is no moisture in the flux or on the work during welding, the quality of submerged-arc weld metal is comparable to that obtained with low-hydrogen electrodes. Packaged flux must be stored in a warm, dry room. Loose flux stored in open containers should be subject to the same drying conditions as low-hydrogen electrodes.

(2) Excessive moisture in the electrode coatings releases hydrogen during welding, and therefore adversely affects the quality of the weld. Since this moisture may be absorbed from the atmosphere, packaged electrodes should be stored in a dry, warm room, and loose electrodes should be stored in drying bins or a holding oven kept at the manufacturer's recommended temperature.

(a) With low-hydrogen electrodes, the coatings have few hydrogen-producing constituents. Special care is taken in manufacturing and packaging these electrodes to maintain a low content of free and combined moisture. If these electrodes absorb much moisture from the atmosphere, they no longer function as low-hydrogen electrodes. The rate of moisture absorption depends on the coating composition and the relative humidity.

(b) The electrode manufacturer should be asked for recommendations about bake time, holding oven temperature, and maximum allowable exposure time for the particular electrode type, quality of weld required, and relative humidity. If this information is unavailable, a general rule is to limit atmospheric exposure to 4 hours for electrodes removed from the bake oven, from holding ovens, or from hermetically sealed metal containers. In critical welding applications or when the relative humidity is 75 percent or higher, the exposure time may have to be reduced to as little as 1/2 hour. Electrodes which have been wet must not be used.

c. The contractor must ensure tack welding and jigging is done properly. Parts to be welded must be held in position before, during, and after welding to keep them correctly aligned and to minimize distortion caused by shrinkage of the weld metal as it cools. To do this, tack welding is frequently used either alone or as a supplement to various jigs, fixtures, and clamps. Tack welds, which are subject to cracking if they are too small, can be a source of defects when subsequent welds are made. Therefore, tack welds should always be inspected and, if cracked, ground out before subsequent welding. Sound tack welds should be ground to a smooth contour that blends evenly into the base metal. This will ease complete melting of the tack weld into the subsequent weld. Before welding is begun, the pieces should be aligned so that afterward the abutting edges of the parts are within the offset tolerances specified in the contract.

d. The contractor must take precautions against adverse weather conditions.

(1) Welding should not be done if the surfaces are wet or covered with snow, ice, or frost. Local preheating of the joint area can be used to dry the joint surfaces. If rain or snow is falling, the joint will have to be sheltered so that the area will stay dry during welding.

(2) Welding will not be done in windy or drafty locations unless curtains or protective screens are used. Most arc welding processes incorporate a shield of gas or vaporized electrode coating to protect the arc and molten weld metal from the air. If the welding is done in a windy or drafty location, this shield can be blown away, and an unsatisfactory weld will result.

(3) Welding should not be done if the temperature at the weld site is below 00 F. If the temperature is between O and 32°F, the joint area should be

preheated to 70 °F or higher for welding and kept at this temperature throughout the welding operation. preheating of structural steel must conform to AWS D1.1.

e. The contractor must insure proper repair welding. Defective welds must be repaired by removing the defects from the weld joint and rewelding the joints. Defects may be removed mechanically by grinding, chipping, or machining, or by arc or flame gouging. A combination of methods is often required. For example, if the defects are removed by flame or arc gouging, the cut surface may need to be cleaned mechanically and smoothed before the repair weld is made.

(1) Flame- or arc-cut surfaces of stainless steel and nickel steel have a heavy scale or oxide coating that must be removed before welding to keep it from affecting the quality of the repair weld. Also, heat from the gouging operation can affect strength by causing metallurgical changes in the weld metal adjacent to the cut surfaces. Therefore, an additional 1/8 inch of metal should be mechanically removed from these cut surfaces.

(2) Defects in aluminum alloys must be removed only by mechanical means.

(3) Extra care must be used when removing cracks from welds. Nondestructive inspection may not indicate the true length of the crack, which may be too narrow to be detected with the test method being used. So, one should remove not only the weld metal in the crack, but also some sound metal at each end of the crack. The amount removed should be twice the base metal thickness or 2 inches, whichever is less at each end of the crack. After the metal is taken out and before repairs, welds should be inspected again to insure that the full length of the crack has been removed.

(4) Repair welding must be done by a qualified welder using only qualified welding procedures. The repair work might be easier with a smaller diameter electrode or filler wire than was used to make the original weld.

f. On critical welds or when requested by inspectors or the contracting officer, the contractor must have a welder or welding operator apply a predetermined identification mark to the completed weld joint. This mark is normally made on the base metal next to the weld metal. Materials may be marked by any method acceptable to the inspector as long as it does not cause notches or sharp discontinuities that could fail under service loading. The identifying mark must remain legible until acceptance of the weld metals or the structure in which the weld is contained. When requested, the welder should apply a mark that will remain legible for the life of the structure.

g. The contractor must set up procedures for preheating, postheating, and stress relieving. The conditions to which a weldment will be exposed during service operations determine the thermal treatment necessary. For a broad coverage of thermal treatment, see the AWS *Welding Handbook,* Volume 1, "Fundamentals of Welding." Since preheating and post-weld heat treatment affect the physical properties of the weld, the procedures must be set up in detail by the contractor or fabricator and included in the welding procedure qualification.

(1) Preheating is the application of heat to a base metal before welding or cutting. Preheating may be used during welding to help complete the welded joint. The need for and temperature of preheating depend on several factors, such as the chemical analysis of the material, degree of restraint of the parts being joined, physical properties at elevated temperatures, material thickness, and ambient temperature.

(a) Preheating may be required or recommended for welding performed under codes or specifications such as those of AWS, ASME, or the American Petroleum Institute (API). However, preheating does not necessarily assure satisfactory completion of the welded joint, and requirements must be suited to the individual materials and applications.

(b) Preheating may vary from a temperature which is warm to the touch of the hand when welding outdoors in winter, to as high as 6000 F when welding highly hardenable steels. When the ambient temperature is less than 32 "F, local preheat of the weld joint area to 700 F is recommended.

(2) Post-weld heat treatment (or postheating) is a general term covering treatments done after welding to restore the properties of the base metal and to produce the desired microstructure in the base and filler metals. Post-weld heat treatment may require normalizing, full annealing, quenching and tempering, or solution and precipitation treatments.

(3) Stress relief heat treatment is the uniform heating of a structure (or part of it) to a temperature below the critical range, but high enough to relieve most of the residual stresses; this is followed by uniform cooling. Stress relieving should not be confused with other post-weld heat treatment processes, which may or may not prevent the need for stress relieving, depending on the maximum temperature attained in the post-weld heat treatment and the rate of cooling from this temperature.

2-3. Inspection requirements

Inspection is done to meet contract quality specifications and to maintain quality control on the welders and welding operators. Effective inspection requires cooperation between the welder or welding operator and the inspector. Inspectors should always encourage the welders and welding operator to check their own work and to report questionable welds or welding procedures. There must also be a mutual understanding between contractor and government supervisory personnel. Inspection costs money, but good inspection often saves more than it costs by reducing expensive, time—consuming rejects or repairs, and by detecting promptly unsatisfactory welding procedures or poor workmanship. Most inspections are to be done by the contractors (fabricators) since they will gain or lose from the quality of the product. They can also take immediate corrective action when defective weldments are found. When contractors do their own inspections, the inspection personnel should be organizationally separate from the production personnel; inspection personnel should answer not to the project superintendent but to a quality control element of the organization. Contractors may employ independent commercial inspection and testing laboratories to perform these services, especially when the contractor's production or quality requirements vary widely. If the contractor has provided reliable inspectors, the government can simply spot check to make sure the inspection methods were adequate. Government inspection can be done either by government personnel or by an independent commercial inspection or testing laboratory. The choice will depend on a number of factors, such as availability of qualified personnel and equipment, length of the project, cost of inspection, location of the project, and criticality of inspection or testing requirements. When qualified government personnel are available, they should do the inspection and testing. This is desirable from the standpoints of administrative control, maintenance of qualified government inspection personnel, and personal interest in the quality of the product. When circumstances require work by a commercial laboratory, these inspectors act as agents for the government.

a. Contractual relations.

(1) Designers, contractors, inspectors, welders, and welding operators should cooperate. The quality of the welding depends largely on the skill of the contractor's personnel, the proper choice of materials, and the adequacy of the welding procedure. The contractor depends on the inspectors for decisions about whether the completed welds are acceptable.

(2) Inspectors should develop a clear understanding of the specified requirements, interpret contract provisions consistently, and avoid either favoring the contractor or making unreasonable demands. In short, they should be absolutely fair to both the government and the contractor.

(3) Although inspectors usually make the final decision about the quality of a weld, they should not take over the role of supervisors for the contractor. Acceptability of welds should not be left to discretion, but be based on meeting the specified requirements. Competent contractor supervision should be provided to see that the welding procedures are being followed and that the requests made by the inspectors are carried out. As much as possible, the inspector should ask the contractor's supervisory personnel to regulate operations, and should not give orders directly to workmen.

(4) A thorough knowledge of the work is the best assurance of a satisfactory job and a good working relationship between the government and the contractor. The inexperienced inspector may unwittingly penalize both contracting parties by unduly emphasizing insignificant but costly details of the work, thus imposing a needless hardship on the contractor with little benefit to the government. At the same time, the inspector might overlook other operations that may be vitally important to the job — for example, overemphasis on the strength of the weld when appearance is most important, and vice versa.

b. Inspection force. On a large project, government inspection of welding operations is assigned to an inspection section headed by an experienced supervisor. This differs from an isolated job of welding where inspection may be the responsibility of one or two individuals. On a large project where the inspection of all welding is given to a specialized team, assignments in the early stages of construction may be arranged so that inexperienced inspectors can watch the actions and decisions of experienced personnel. This procedure will help train a competent team that will operate efficiently at a later stage of work. This approach is not possible, however, on small projects with only one inspector. Only experienced construction personnel should be assigned in such cases.

c. Inspector's duties. The inspector must examine in detail each phase of the welding operation to make sure the work is being done right. The inspector must observe such requirements as procedure and welder qualifications, joint design and preparation, alignment, electrode size and type, welding equipment, and technique. When an assignment is rotated, a new inspector must learn about the procedures being followed and the status of welding and inspection   before   assuming   inspection responsibility.

d. Supervision. Good supervision of inspectors is important to satisfactory welding operations on a large project. Even the most experienced inspector can do little unless properly instructed in the work and given the fullest support in dealings with welding personnel.   The supervisor must clarify the responsibilities of each part of the organization and outline the limits of each inspector's authority. The supervisor should tell the inspector about all decisions on acceptance requirements and other issues.

It is good supervisory practice to circulate memoranda outlining all project decisions made by those in authority and summarizing matters which inspectors can still decide with some flexibility. Before decisions are made about construction methods, the opinions of the inspectors assigned to the work should be considered. Occasional meetings between inspectors and supervisors to discuss any job problems, practices,   and requirements are helpful and often necessary.

CHAPTER 3

WELDING PROCESSES

3-1. General

This chapter contains general requirements for welding processes that may be used for the applications covered in paragraph 1-2.

3-2. Processes

a. The welding processes covered by this design manual are as follows:

   (1) Shielded metal-arc (SMAW)
   (2) Gas metal-arc (GMAW)

     (a) Free-flight transfer
     (b) Pulsed-current out-of-position welding
     (c) Short circuiting

   (3) Flux-cored arc welding (FCAW)
   (4) Gas tungsten-arc (GTAW)
   (5) Submerged-arc (SAW)
   (6) Exothermic (Thermit)
   (7) Arc stud (STUD)

b. Basically, in the electric welding processes, an arc is produced between an electrode and the work piece (base metal). The arc is formed by passing

current from the electrode to the work piece through a gap. The current melts the base metal and the electrode if it is a consumable type, creating a molten pool. On solidifying, the weld is formed. An alternate method employs a nonconsumable electrode such as a tungsten rod. In this case, the weld is formed by melting and solidifying the base metal at the joint. In some instances, additional metal is required and is added to the molten pool from a filler rod.

c. Electrodes which become the deposited weld metal are available in various diameters and lengths. In welding, the molten pool must be protected from the ambient atmosphere to prevent contamination. There are three ways to do this. Two involve a flux; in one, the flux is part of the electrode, either as a coating on the wire or as the core of a hollow wire. The second method uses a granulated flux that is applied separately before welding. The third method involves a gas such as helium, argon, or carbon dioxide. In addition to shielding, the flux may

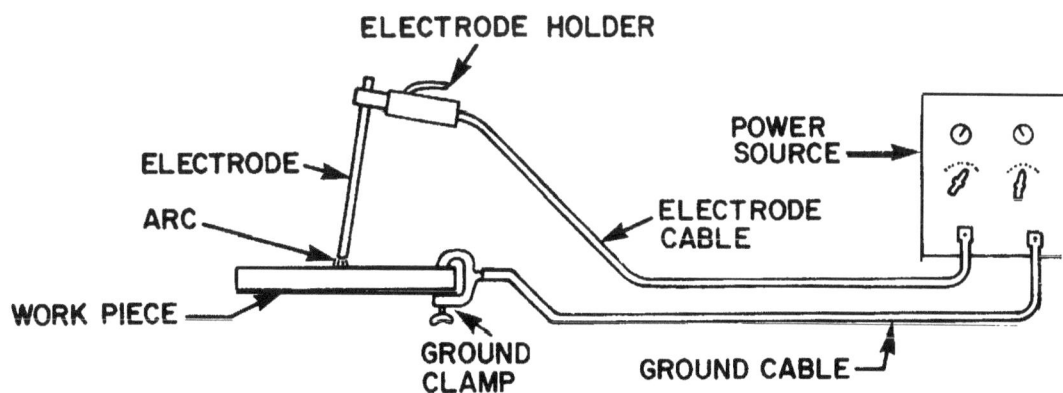

Figure 3-1. Schematic drawing of SMAW equipment.

function as a deoxidizer to purify the deposited metal or to form slag to protect the weld metal from oxidation. The flux may contain ionizing elements to provide smoother operation, alloying elements to provide higher strength, and iron powder to increase production rates. The selection of electrodes for a specific job can be based on the following eight factors:

(1) Base metal strength properties
(2) Base metal composition
(3) Welding position
(4) Welding current
(5) Joint design and fit-up
(6) Thickness and shape of base metal
(7) Service conditions and/or specifications
(8) Production efficiency and job conditions

The AWS publishes a group of specifications for filler metals (electrodes) and recommends the welding process for which they are to be used. In addition, AWS D1.1 describes the welding procedures to be used with the various welding processes.

d. Welding material — electrodes, welding wire, and fluxes — must produce satisfactory welds when used by a qualified welder or welding operator using qualified welding procedures. Welding materials must comply with the applicable requirements of AWS D1.1, ASME Boiler and Pressure Vessel Code, Section II, or other requirements in the contract specifications.

3-3. Shielded metal-arc (SMAW)

This is the most widely used method for general welding application; it may also be referred to as metallic-arc, manual metal-arc, or stick-electrode welding.

a. Advantages. The SMAW process can be used for welding most structural and alloy steels. These include low-carbon or mild steels; low-alloy, heat-treatable steels; and high-alloy steels such as stainless steels. SMAW is used for joining common nickel alloys and can be used for copper and aluminum alloys. This welding process can be used in all positions — flat, vertical, horizontal, or overhead — and requires only the simplest equipment. Thus, SMAW lends itself very well to field work (fig 3-l).

b. Disadvantages. SMAW is clearly inferior to GMAW if one compares the cost of the time and materials needed to deposit the weld metal. SMAW deposits the weld more slowly than does GMAW. In addition, slag removal, unused electrode stubs, and spatter add a lot to the cost of SMAW; the latter two items account for about 44 percent of the consumed electrodes. Another potential cost is the entrapment of slag in the form of inclusions which may have to be removed.

c. Process principles. The SMAW process produces an arc between the base metal and the electrode. The electrode, put in a hand-held clamp, is

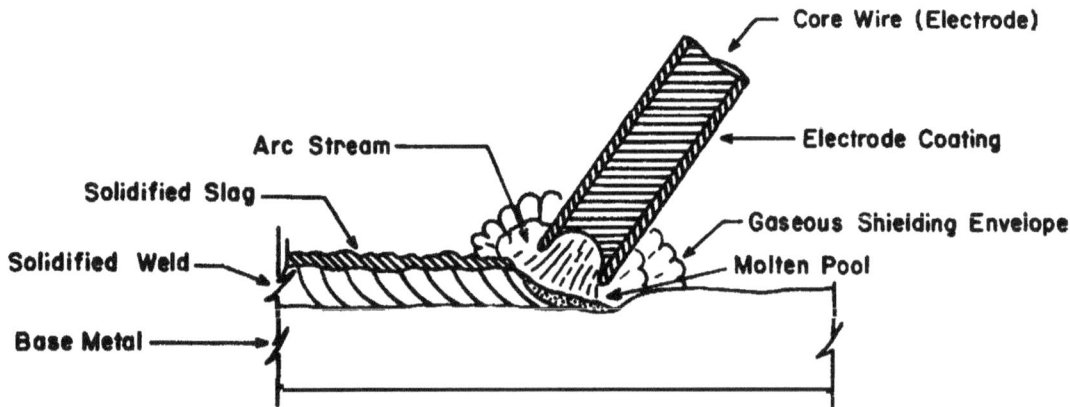

Reprinted from MIL HDBK 56, Materials and Material Processes Series -- Arc Welding, Department of Defense, 1968 (noncopyrighted).

Figure 3-2. Schematic diagram of the SMAW process.

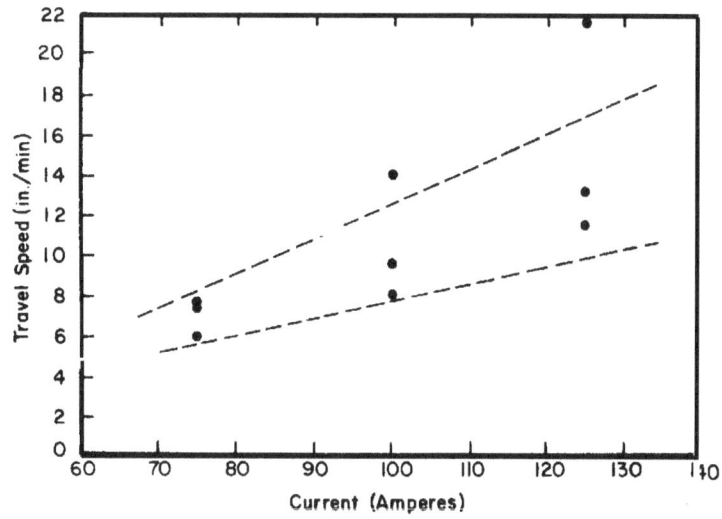

Reprinted from CERL TR-M-302, Weldability Characteristics of Construction Steels A36, A514, and A516, U.S. Army Construction Engineering Research Laboratory, 1981 (noncopyrighted).

Figure 3-3. Travel speed limits for current levels used for 1/8-inch-diameter E6010 SMAW electrode. Dashed lines show travel speed limits as determined by amount of undercut and bead shape.

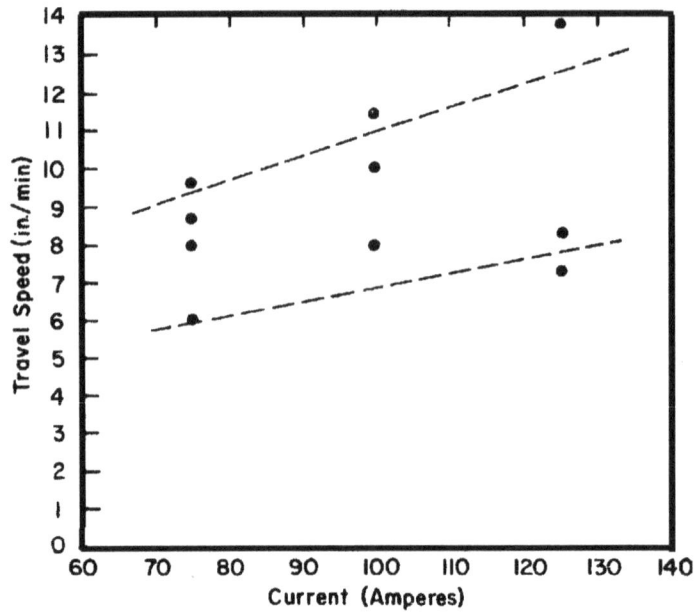

Reprinted from CERL TR-M-302, Weldability
Characteristics of Construction Steels
A36, A514, and A516, U.S. Army Construction
Engineering Research Laboratory, 1981
(noncopyrighted).

Figure 3-4. Travel speed limits for current levels used for 1/8-inch-diameter E6011 SMAW electrode. Dashed lines show travel speed limits as determined by amount of undercut and bead shape.

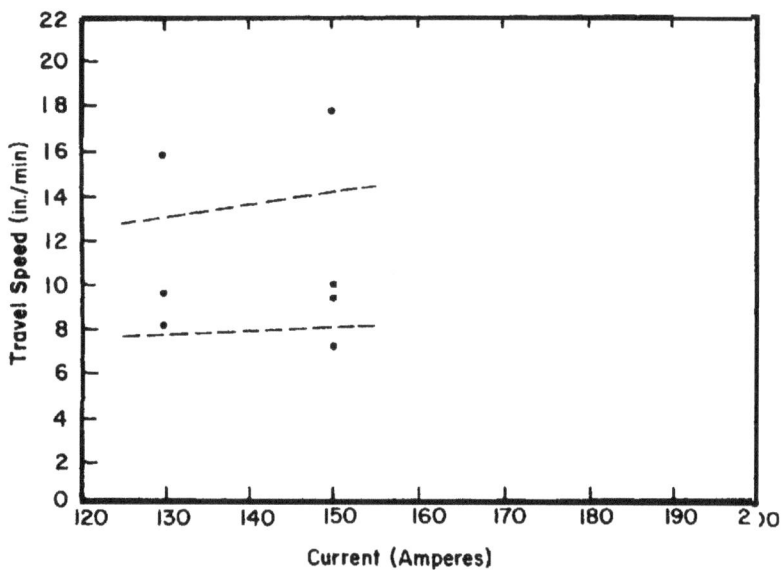

Reprinted from CERL TR-M-302, Weldability
Characteristics of Construction Steels
A36, A514, and A51G, U.S. Army Construction
Engineering Research Laboratory, 1981
(noncopyrighted).

Figure 3-5. Travel speed limits for current levels used for 1/8-inch-diameter E6013 SMAW electrode. Dashed lines show travel speed limits as determined by amount of undercut and bead shape.

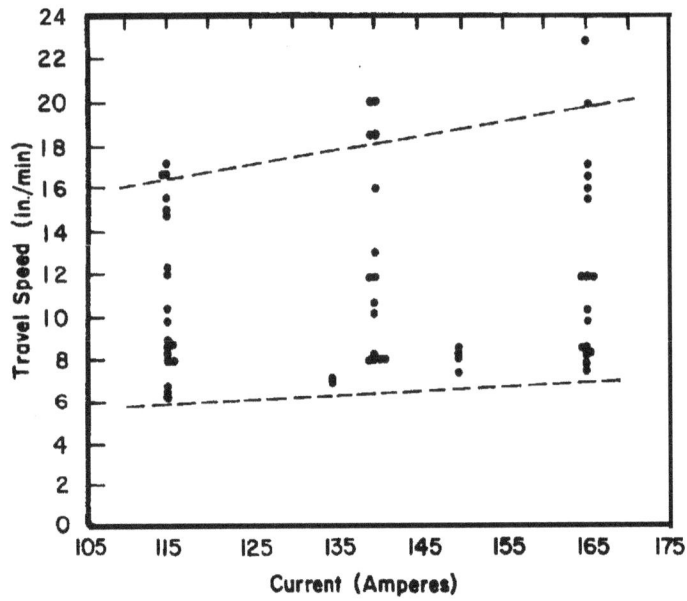

Reprinted from CERL TR-M-302, Weldability
Characteristics of Construction Steels
A36, A514, and A516, U.S. Army Construction
Engineering Research Laboratory, 1981
(noncopyrighted).

Figure 3-6. Travel speed limits for current levels used for 1/8-inch-diameter E7018 SMAW electrode Dashed lines show travel speed limits as determined by amount of undercut and bead shape.

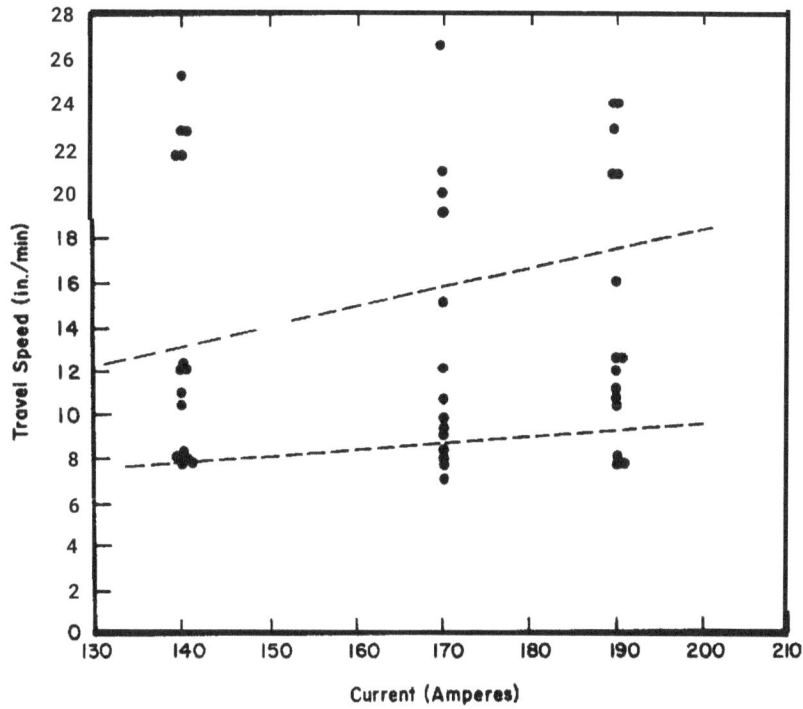

Reprinted from CERL TR-M-302, Weldability
Characteristics of Construction Steels
A36, A514, and A516, U.S. Army Construction
Engineering Research Laboratory, 1981
(noncopyrighted).

Figure 3-7. Travel speed limits for current levels used for 1/8-inch-diameter E7024 SMAW electrode. Dashed lines show travel speed limits as determined by amount of undercut and bead shape.

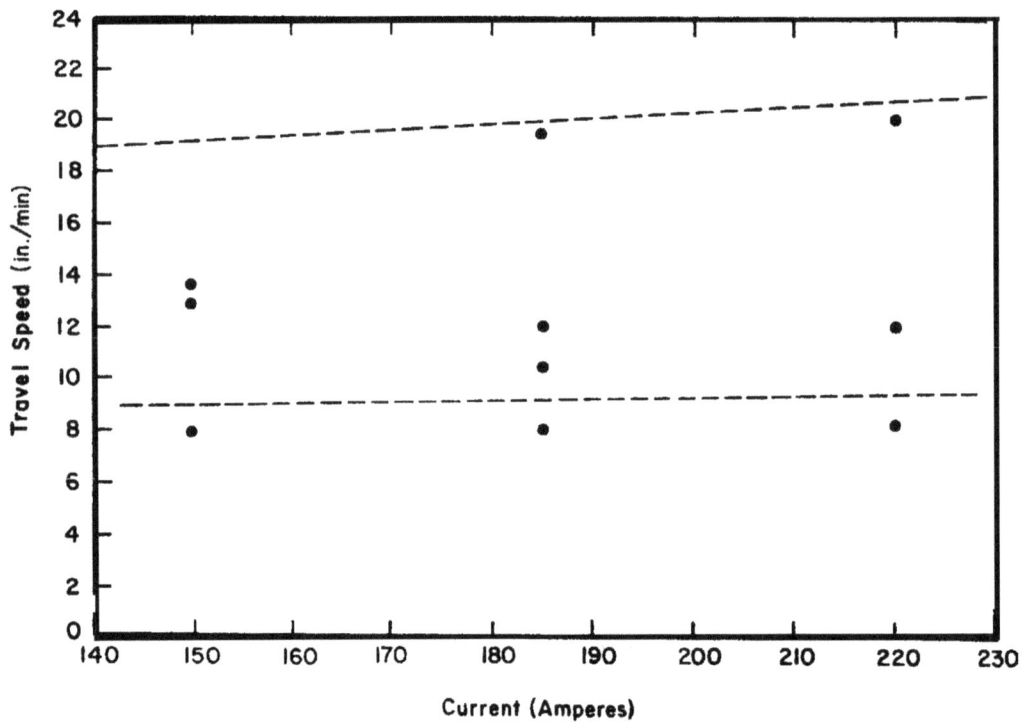

Reprinted from CERL TR-M-302, Weldability
Characteristics of Construction Steels
A36, A514, and A516, U.S. Army Construction
Engineering Research Laboratory, 1981
(noncopyrighted).

Figure 3-8. Travel speed limits for current levels used for 5/32-inch-diameter E8018 SMAW electrode. Dashed lines show travel speed limits as determined by amount of undercut and bead shape.

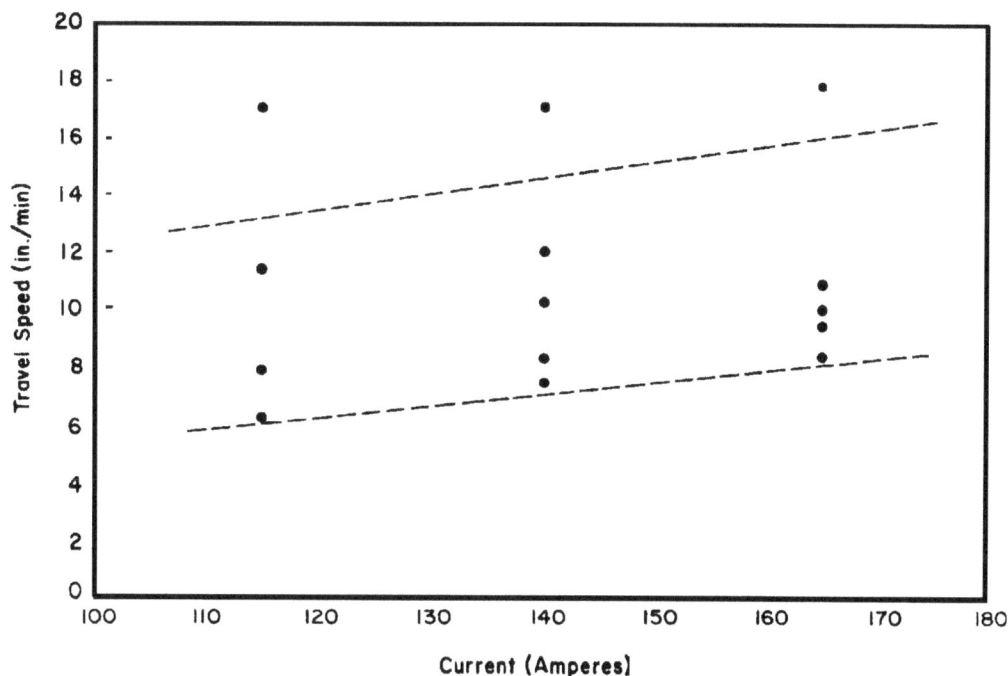

Figure 3-9. Travel speed limits for current levels used for 1/8-inch-diameter E11018 SMAW electrode. Dashed lines show travel speed limits as determined by amount of undercut and bead shape.

struck against the base metal and withdrawn to create a gap. The molten portion of the electrode fuses into the molten pool of the base metal, producing the weld (fig 3-2). Since SMAW is a manual process, the operator is primarily responsible for quality of the weld. Most of the melted electrode metal is transferred to the work piece; the rest is thrown free of the weld as spatter or is vaporized. Of that vaporized, some escapes into the surrounding air, becomes oxidized, and appears as smoke or fumes. The electrode used for SMAW has a special covering which serves several purposes. Part of the covering contains gas-producing compounds that, when heated, produce a gaseous envelope around the arc that displaces air and stabilizes the arc. The covering also protects the molten weld metal from contamination by air. Without this stabilization, the arc would be erratic, would often short out, and generally would be hard to control. Different gas-producing compounds are used in the coating, depending on the type of current — alternating (AC) or direct

(DC). The covering also contains slag-forming materials that mix with the molten weld metal and pick up impurities from the weld metal. This cleaning action improves the quality of the weld. Most of the electrode coating does not become vaporized but instead is melted by the arc heat and forms a molten slag cover over the top of the weld bead. This molten slag cover helps to control the shape of the weld bead. It also helps to hold the molten weld metal in place during out-of-position welding (i.e., welding in the overhead, vertical, or horizontal positions). Chapters 4 and 5 discuss the numbering system, color coding, flux composition, and other data concerning welding electrodes. In shielded metal-arc welding, five distinct forces are responsible for the transfer of molten filler metal and molten slag to the base metal.

(1) Gravity. Gravity is the principal force which accounts for the transfer of filler metal in flat position welding. In other positions, the surface tension is unable to retain much molten metal and slag in the

crater. Therefore, smaller electrodes must be used to avoid excessive loss of weld metal and slag.

(2) Gas expansion. Gases are produced by the burning and volatilization of the electrode coating and are expanded by the heat of the boiling electrode tip. The coating extending beyond the metal tip of the electrode controls the direction of the rapid gas expansion and directs the molten metal globule into the weld metal pool formed in the base metal.

(3) Electromagnetic forces. The electrode tip is an electrical conductor, as is the molten metal globule at the tip. Therefore, the globule is affected by magnetic forces acting at 90 degrees to the direction of the current flow. These forces produce a pinching effect on the metal globules and speed up the separation of the molten metal from the end of the electrode. This is particularly helpful in transferring metal in horizontal, vertical, and overhead position welding.

(4) Electrical forces. The force produced by the voltage across the arc pulls the small, pinched-off globule of metal, regardless of the position of welding. This force is especially helpful when one uses

direct-current, straight-polarity, mineral-coated electrodes, which do not produce large volumes of gas.

(5) Surface tension. The force which keeps the filler metal and slag globules in contact with molten base or weld metal in the crater is known as surface tension. It helps to retain the molten metal in horizontal, vertical, and overhead welding, and to determine the shape of weld contours.

d. Equipment, The equipment needed for shielded metal-arc welding is much less complex than that needed for other arc welding processes. Manual welding equipment includes a power source (transformer, DC generator, AC generator, or DC rectifier), electrode holder, cables, connectors, chipping hammer, wire brush, and electrodes.

e. Welding parameters. Welding voltage, current, and travel speed are very important to the quality of the deposited SMAW bead. Table 3-1 shows voltage limits for some SMAW electrodes. The current limits are shown in the appendix to AWS A5.1. Figures 3-3 through 3-9 show the travel speed limits for the electrodes listed in table 3-1.

a. Projected
(Spray)

b. Repelled
(by CO_2)

c. Gravitational
(Globular)

Reprinted from MIL HDBK 56, Materials and Material Processes Series -- Arc Welding, Department of Defense, 1968 (noncopyrighted).

Figure 3-10. Three types of free-flight metal transfer in a welding arc.

WIRE DRIVE MAY BE LOCATED
IN WELDING GUN HANDLE
OR AT WIRE REEL

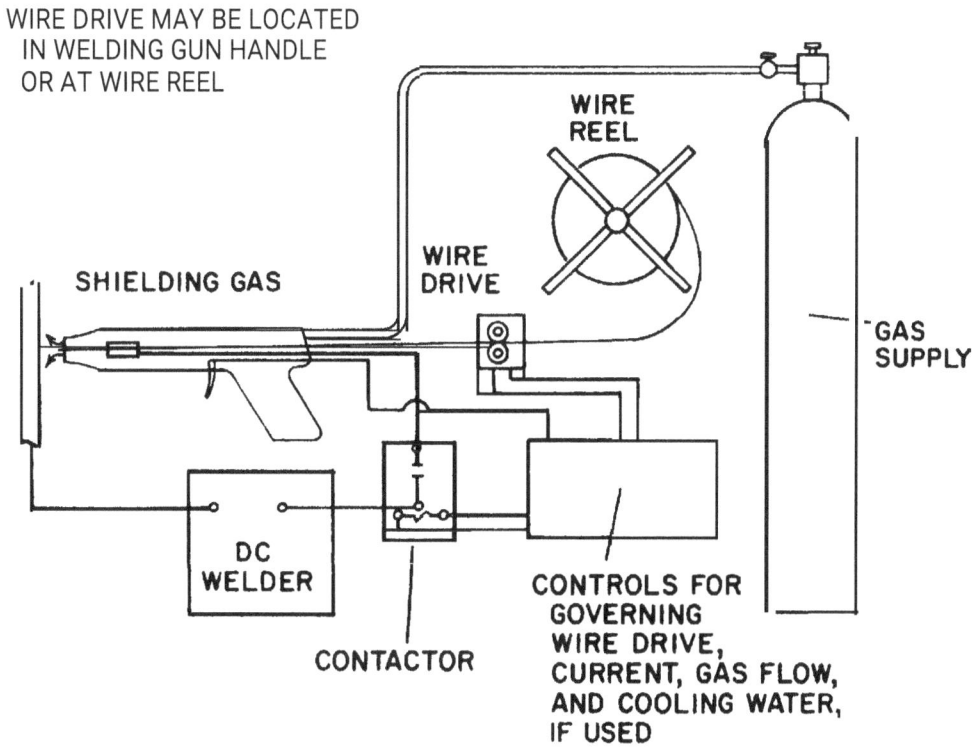

Reprinted from MIL HDBK 56, Materials and
Material Processes Series -- Arc Welding,
Department of Defense, 1968 (noncopyrighted).

Figure 3-11. The GMAW processes.

Table 3-1. Established voltage limits

Electrode[a]	Voltage limits, V
E6010	28 to 32
E6011	28 to 32
E6013	22 to 26
E7018	25 to 28
E7024	26 to 32
E8018	22 to 28
E11018	25 to 30

"Note all electrodes 1/8-inch diameter except E8018, which is 5/32-inch diameter.

3-4. Gas metal-arc (GMAW)

GMAW is a process in which an electric arc is established between a solid, consumable, spool-fed electrode and the work piece. The arc, electrode tip, and molten weld metal are shielded from the atmosphere by a gas. This welding process has been commonly called metal-inert-gas welding (MIG). There are two main types of metal transfer: free flight and short circuiting. Free-flight transfer can be projected or spray, repelled, and gravitational or globular. These three forms of free-flight transfer are basically for flat position welding (fig 3-10). A modification of free-flight transfer is pulsed current, which can be used in all welding positions. The short-circuiting transfer, sometimes called short-arc, uses a low current and is for welding thin materials in all positions. All the GMAW processes use basically the same equipment, as shown in figure 3-11. AWS D1.1 describes electrodes, shielding gas, and welding procedures for GMAW using single electrodes.

a. Free-flight transfer gas metal-arc welding.

(1) Advantages. The major advantage of free-flight transfer welding is that high-quality welds can be produced much faster than with SMAW or GTAW. Since a flux is not used, there is no chance for the entrapment of slag in the weld metal. The gas shield protects the arc so that there is very little loss of alloying elements as the metal transfers across the arc. Only minor weld spatter is produced, and this is easily removed. The free-flight process is versatile and can be successfully used with a wide variety of metals and alloys: aluminum, copper, magnesium, nickel, and many of their alloys, as well as iron and most of its alloys. The process can be operated in several ways, including semi- and fully automatic. GMAW is widely used by many industries for welding a broad variety of materials, parts, and structures.

(2) Disadvantages. The major disadvantage of free-flight transfer is that it cannot be used in vertical or overhead welding due to the high heat input and the fluidity of the weld puddle. In addition, the equipment is complex compared with that for the SMAW process.

(3) Process principles. In free-flight transfer, the liquid drops that form at the tip of the consumable electrode are detached and travel freely across the space between the electrode and work piece before plunging into the weld pool (fig 3-10). When the transfer is gravitational, the drops are detached by gravity alone and fall slowly through the arc column, In the projected type of transfer, other forces give the drop an initial acceleration and project it independently of gravity toward the weld pool, During repelled transfer, forces act on the liquid drop and give it an initial velocity directly away from the weld pool. The gravitational and projected modes of free-flight metal transfer may occur in the gas metal-arc welding of steel, nickel alloys, or aluminum alloys using a direct-current, electrode-positive (reverse polarity) arc and properly selected types of shielding gases. At low currents, wires of these alloys melt slowly. A large spherical drop forms at the tip and is detached when the force due to gravity exceeds that of surface tension. As the current increases, the electromagnetic force becomes significant and the total separating force increases. The rate at which drops are formed and detached also increases. At a certain current, a change occurs in the character of the arc and metal transfer. The arc column, previously bell-shaped or spherical and having relatively low brightness, becomes narrower and more conical and has a bright central core. The droplets that form at the wire tip become elongated due to magnetic pressure and are detached at a much higher rate. When carbon dioxide is used as the shielding gas, the type of metal transfer is much different. At low and medium reversed-polarity currents, the drop appears to be repelled from the work electrode and is eventually detached while moving away from the work piece and weld pool, This causes an excessive amount of spatter. At higher currents, the transfer is less irregular because other forces, primarily electrical, overcome the repelling forces. Direct current reversed-polarity is recommended for the GMAW process. Straight polarity and alternating current can be used, but require precautions such as a special coating on the electrode wire or special shield gas mixtures.

(4) Equipment. The equipment needed for solid-wire, free-flight transfer welding includes a power supply, a welding gun, a mechanism for feeding the electrode filler wire, and a set of controls (fig 3-11). Two types of power sources are used for free-flight transfer welding — constant current or constant voltage. Motor generator or DC rectifier power sources of either type may be used. Both

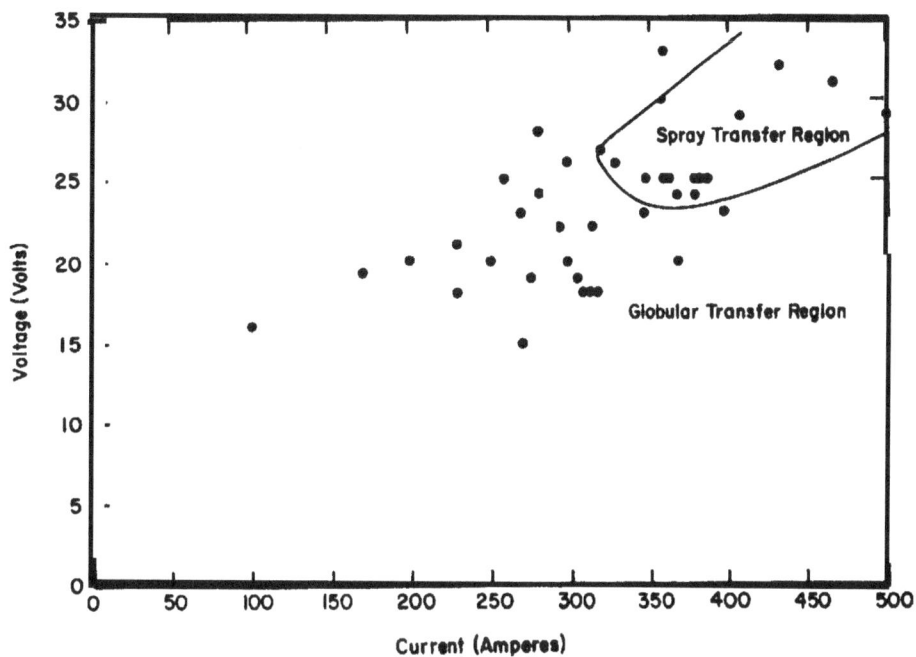

Reprinted from CERL TR-M-302, <u>Weldability</u>
<u>Characteristics of Construction Steels</u>
<u>A36, A514, and A516</u>, U.S. Army Construction
Engineering Research Laboratory, 1981
(noncopyrighted).

Figure 3-12. Voltage versus current for E70S-2 1/16-inch-diameter electrode and shield gas of argon with 2-percent oxygen addition.

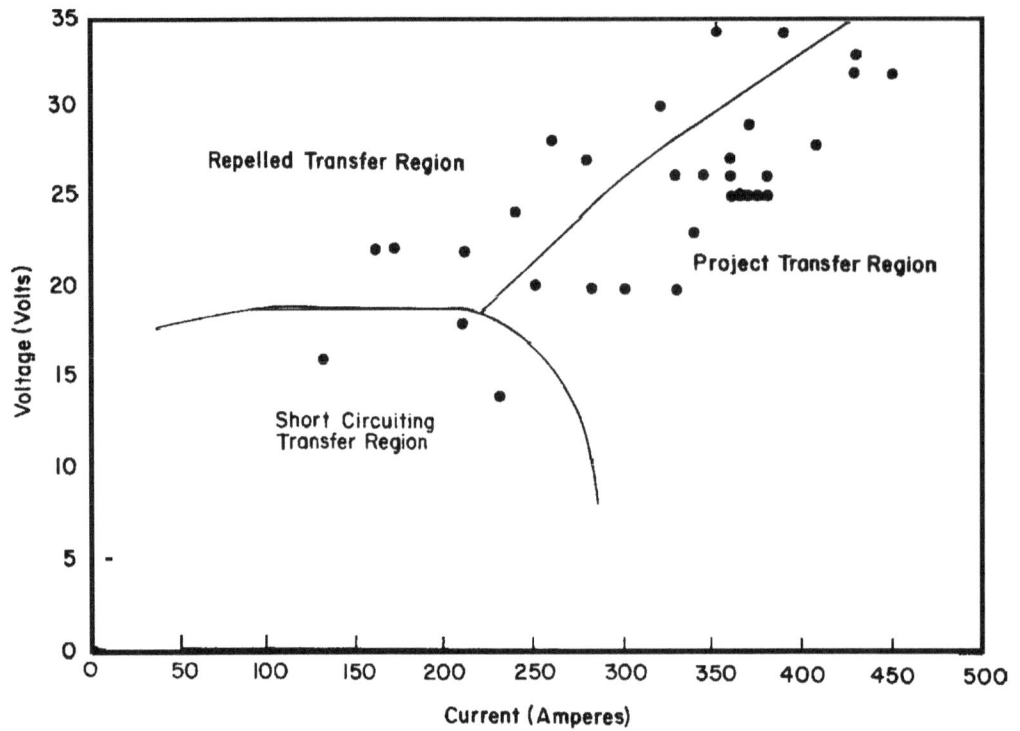

Reprinted from CERL TR-M-302, Weldability Characteristics of Construction Steels A36, A514, and A516, U.S. Army Construction Engineering Research Laboratory, 1981 (noncopyrighted).

Figure 3-13. Voltage versus current for E70S-2 1/16-inch-diameter electrode and carbon dioxide shield gas.

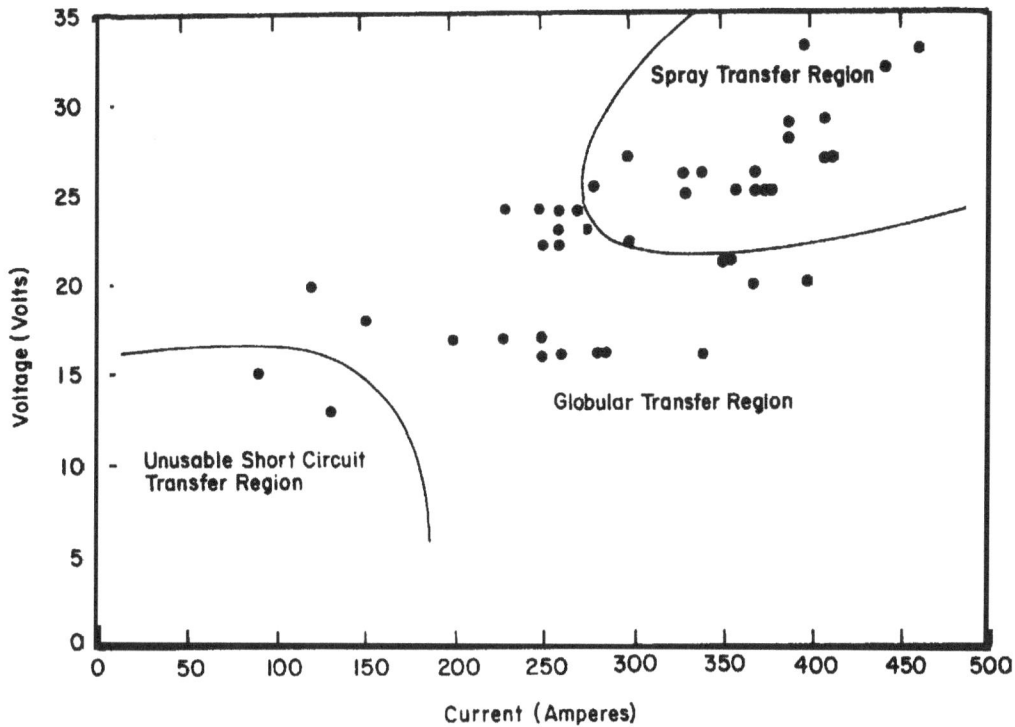

Reprinted from CERL TR-M-302, Weldability
Characteristics of Construction Steels
A36, A514, and A516, U.S. Army Construction
Engineering Research Laboratory, 1981
(noncopyrighted).

Figure 3-14. Voltage versus current for E70S-3 1/16-inch-diameter electrode and shield gas of argon with 2-percent oxygen addition.

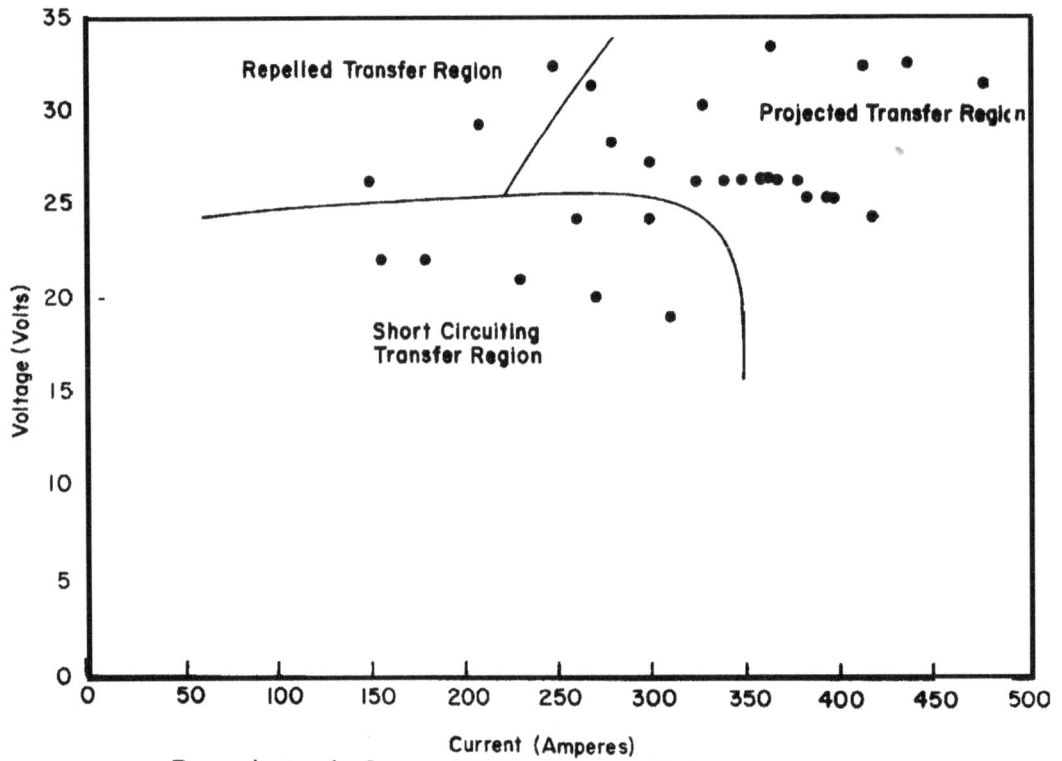

Reprinted from CERL TR-M-302, Weldability
Characteristics of Construction Steels
A36, A514, and A516, U.S. Army Construction
Engineering Research Laboratory, 1981
(noncopyrighted).

Figure 3-15. Voltage versus current for E70S-3 1/16-inch-diameter electrode and carbon dioxide shield gas.

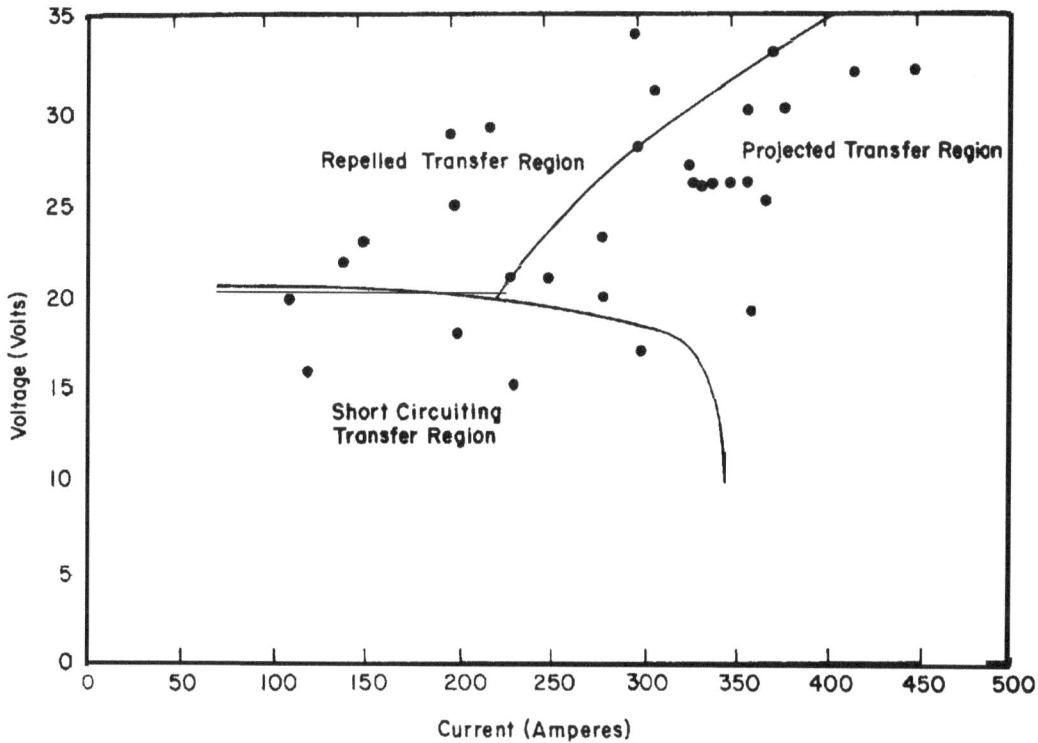

Reprinted from CERL TR-M-302, Weldability
Characteristics of Construction Steels
A36, A514, and A516, U.S. Army Construction
Engineering Research Laboratory, 1981
(noncopyrighted).

Figure 3-16. Voltage versus current for E70S-4 1/16-inch-diameter electrode and carbon dioxide shield gas.

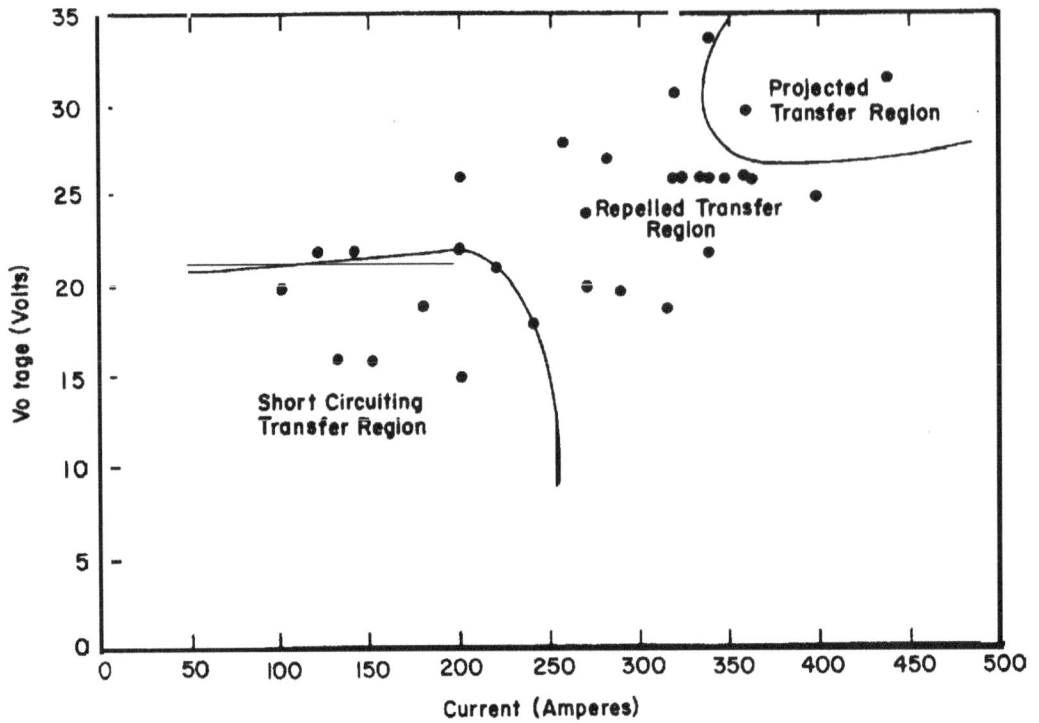

Reprinted from CERL TR-M-302, Weldability
Characteristics of Construction Steels
A36, A514, and A516, U.S. Army Construction
Engineering Research Laboratory, 1981
(noncopyrighted).

Figure 3-17. Voltage versus current for E70S-6 1/16-inch-diameter electrode and carbon dioxide shield gas.

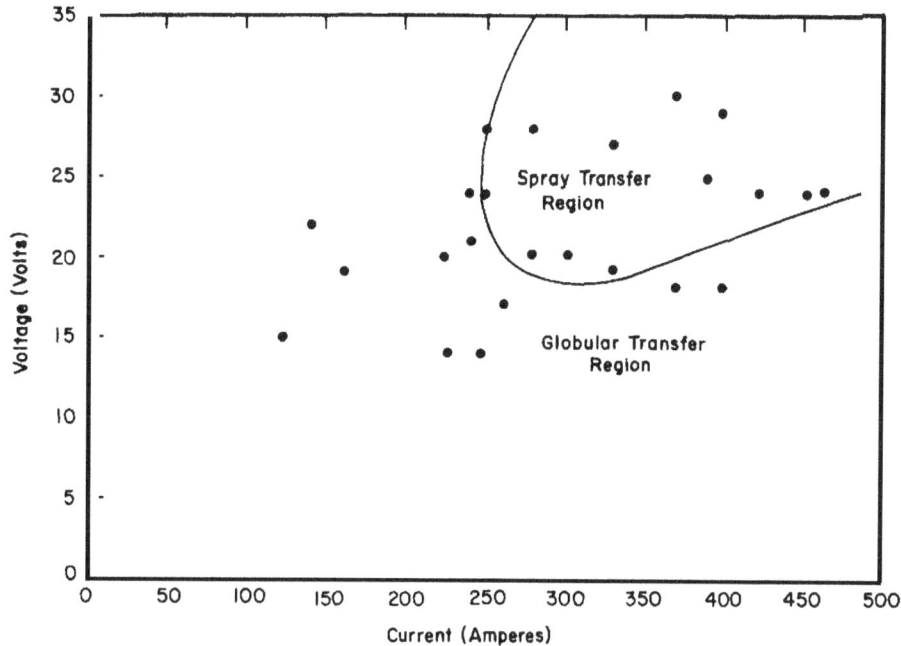

Reprinted from CERL TR-M-302, Weldability Characteristics of Construction Steels A36, A514, and A516, U.S. Army Construction Engineering Research Laboratory, 1981 (noncopyrighted).

Figure 3-18. Voltage versus current for E110S 1/16-inch-diameter electrode and shield gas of argon with 2-percent oxygen addition.

manual and automatic welding guns are available. The manual welding guns have many designs. All the manual guns have a nozzle for directing the shielding gas around the arc and over the weld puddle. The filler wire passes through a copper contact tube in the gun, where it picks up the welding current. Some manual welding guns contain the wire-driving mechanism within the gun itself. other guns require that the wire-feeding mechanism be located at the spool of wire, which is some distance from the gun. In this case, the wire is driven through a flexible conduit to the welding gun. Another manual gun design combines feed mechanisms within the gun and at the wire supply itself. Argon is the shielding gas used most often. Small amounts of oxygen (2 to 5 percent) frequently are added to the shielding gas when steel is welded. This stabilizes the arc and promotes a better wetting action, producing a more uniform weld bead and reducing undercut. Carbon dioxide is also used as a shielding gas because it is cheaper than argon and argon-oxygen mixtures.

Electrodes designed to be used with carbon dioxide shielding gas require extra deoxidizers in their formulation because in the heat of the arc, the carbon dioxide dissociates to carbon monoxide and oxygen, which can cause oxidation of the weld metal.

(5) Welding parameters. Figures 3-12 through 3-18 show the relationship between the voltage and current levels, and the type of transfer across the arcs.

b. Pulsed-current GMAW process.

(1) Advantages. This process is useful when low heat input is required — when one is working with thin materials or doing out-of-position welding, for example. In the lower heat-input range, pulsed current has the advantage of the continous projected spray-transfer process. High-quality welds can be produced in mild and low-alloy steels. In the welding of aluminum, larger diameter wires can be used; welds with less porosity are produced because there is less hydrogen and oxygen pickup on the wire surface.

3-19

(2) Disadvantages. The major disadvantage of this process is the complex power supply required in addition to the GMAW wire feeder and welding torch.

(3) Process principles. Pulsed-current GMAW is a modification of the process used to obtain spray-type transfer with average current levels in the globular-transfer range. This process provides a higher ratio of heat input to metal deposition rate than the short-circuiting process. Pulsed-current GMAW operates at heat inputs between those used for spray transfer and short-circuiting transfer, with some overlap in the ranges. In this process, the current is pulsed back and forth between projected-transfer and gravitational-transfer ranges by electronically switching the current level back and forth between them. Figure 3-19 shows the current output-wave form and metal-transfer sequence. Pulsed-current welding is also known by the trade name "pulsed-arc."

(4) Equipment. The power sources for pulsed current combine a three-phase, full-wave transformer-rectifier power supply, and a single-phase, half-wave pulse unit. These units are connected in parallel, but are electronically switched in operation to give the output waveform shown in figure 3-19.

Standard GMAW wire feeder and torches are used in this process.

c. Short-circuiting transfer GMAW welding.

(1) Advantages. The short-circuiting process is widely used for quickly welding thin materials (up to 1/4 inch) in all positions; it causes little distortion and few metallurgical defects. This process is used on carbon and low-alloy steels, and less often on stainless steel and aluminum; it is also used for out-of-position welding of thicker materials.

(2) Disadvantages. Generally, welds made with the short-circuiting process are of slightly poorer quality than those produced by the spray-transfer method. This may not cause trouble if high-quality welds are not required.

(3) Process principles. The short-circuiting transfer variation of the GMAW process is generally similar to spray-transfer welding. The main difference is the way the molten metal is transferred from the end of the electrode wire to the weld puddle. In spray-transfer welding, droplets are transferred through the arc. With the short-circuiting process, metal transfer occurs during repetitive short circuits caused when the molten metal from the electrode contacts the weld puddle. The welding current is well below the transition level required for spray

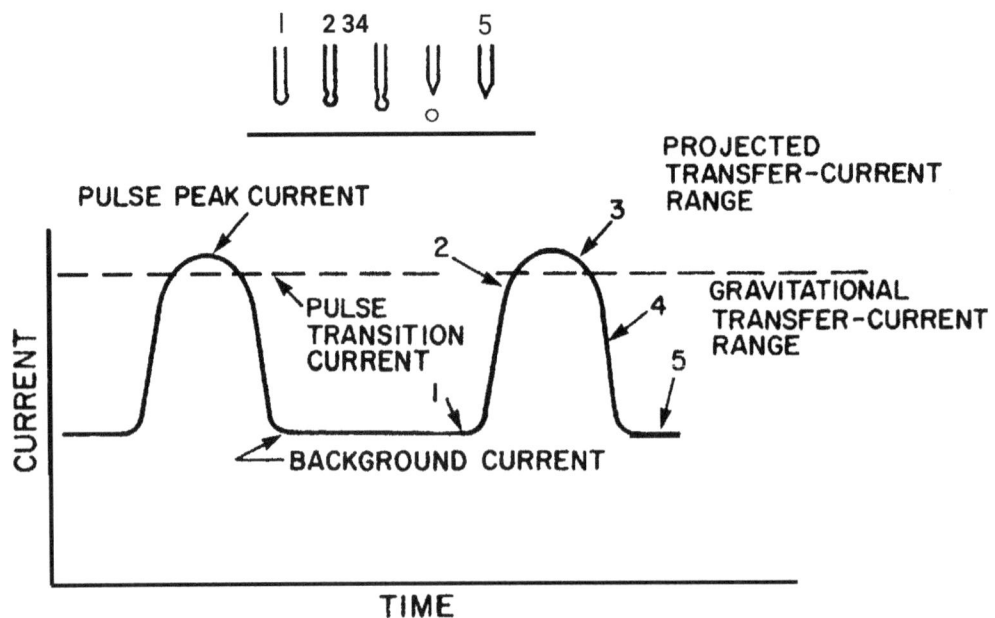

Reprinted from MIL HDBK 56, Materials and Material Processes Series -- Arc Welding, Department of Defense, 1968 (noncopyrighted).

Figure 3-19. The output current wave form of the pulsed-current power supply. The metal transfer sequence is also shown.

transfer. As the end of the filler wire melts, it forms a ball (fig 3-20). This becomes larger until it touches the weld puddle, extinguishing the arc and creating a short circuit. The arc length is deliberately kept short so that the metal ball touches the puddle before it separates from the end of the filler wire. When the short circuit occurs, the welding current increases rapidly, causing the drop of molten metal to be "pinched" from the end of the filler wire. The arc is reinitiated and the process repeated. The short-circuiting action is very rapid; as many as 200 short circuits per second may occur. This process is also known as "short arc, " dip-transfer, or fine wire welding,

(4) Equipment. Short-circuiting transfer welding uses the same constant voltage equipment as does spray transfer. The power source must have a device that inserts a variable but controlled amount of inductance into the electrical circuit. This inductance controls the rate of current increase when the short circuit occurs and permits the arc to restart without weld-metal spatter.

(a) Short-circuiting welding requires a smaller diameter filler wire (0.030-inch diameter, for example) than is generally used for spray-transfer welding.

(b) The shielding gas used for short-circuiting welding depends on the metal being welded. Argon, helium, or mixtures of these are used for welding aluminum. Carbon dioxide, a mixture of carbon dioxide and argon, or argon with a small oxygen addition is used when welding mild or low-alloy steel. For stainless steel, argon with oxygen or carbon dioxide additions is used.

3-5. Flux-cored arc welding (FCAW)

Flux-cored, tubular-electrode welding has evolved from the GMAW process to improve arc action, metal transfer, weld-metal properties, and weld appearance.

a. Advantages. The major advantages of flux-cored welding are reduced cost and higher deposition rates than either SMAW or solid wire GMAW. The cost is less for flux-cored electrodes because the alloying agents are in the flux, not in the steel filler wire as they are with solid electrodes. Flex-cored welding is ideal where bead appearance is important and no machining of the weld is required. Flex-cored welding without carbon dioxide shielding can be used for most mild steel construction applications, The resulting welds have higher strength but less ductility than those for which carbon dioxide shielding is used. There is less porosity and greater penetration of the weld with carbon dioxide shielding, The flux-cored process has increased tolerances for scale and dirt; there is less weld spatter than with solid-wire GMAW.

b. Disadvantages. Most low-alloy or mild-steel electrodes of the flux-cored type are more sensitive to changes in welding conditions than are SMAW electrodes. This sensitivity, called voltage tolerance, can be decreased if a shielding gas is used, or if the slag-forming components of the core material are increased. A constant-potential power source and constant-speed electrode feeder are needed to maintain a constant arc voltage.

c. Process principles. The flux-core welding wire, or electrode, is a hollow tube filled with a mixture of deoxidizers, fluxing agents, metal powders, and ferro alloys, as shown in figure 3-21. The closure seam, which appears as a fine line, is the only visible

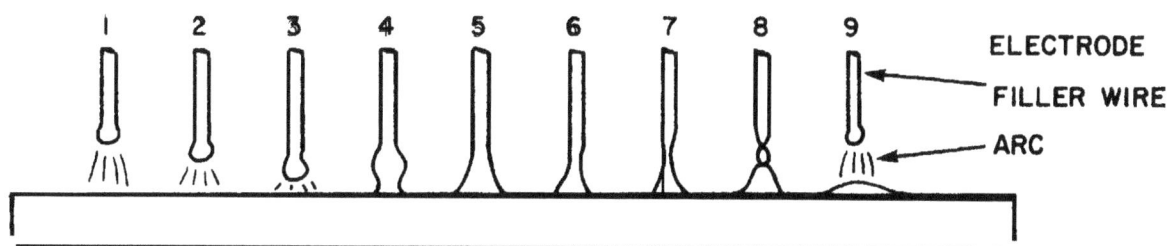

Figure 3-20. Steps in short-circuiting metal transfer

difference between flux-cored wires and solid cold-drawn wire. Flux-cored electrode welding can be done in two ways: carbon dioxide gas can be used with the flux to provide additional shielding, or the flux core alone can provide all the shielding gas and slagging materials. The carbon dioxide gas shield produces a deeply penetrating arc and usually provides better weld than is possible without an external gas shield.

d. Equipment. The equipment and controls for the flux-core process are similar to, and sometimes the same as, those used in the stray-transfer method. The unit consists of a constant-speed wire-drive system, water- or air-cooled welding torch, and a constant-potential DC unit with a 100-percent duty cycle.

3-6. Gas tungsten-arc (GTAW)

The GTAW process uses a nonconsumable electrode and an inert shielding gas. This process is also known as TIG (tungsten inert gas) and by the trade name "Heliarc." GTAW is similar to other arc-welding processes in that the heat is generated by an arc between a nonconsumable electrode and the work piece, but the equipment and the electrode type distinguish GTAW from the other arc welding processes.

a. Advantages. The GTAW process is the most popular method for welding aluminum, stainless steel, and nickel base alloys. It produces top quality welds in almost all metals and alloys used in industry. The process provides more precise control of the weld than any other arc welding method because the arc heat and filler metal are independently controlled, Visibility is excellent because no smoke or fumes are produced during welding; there is no slag or splatter that must be cleaned between passes or on a completed weld, GTAW is usually considered one of the most versatile processes because it produces the highest quality welds in any position or configuration, The final major advantage is reduced distortion in the weld joint because of the concentrated heat source. This is one of the best precautions that can be taken to prevent weld cracking or locked-up stresses.

b. Disadvantages. The GTAW process is expensive because the arc travel speed and weld metal deposition rates are lower than with some other methods. In addition, it is less advantageous to use GTAW on heavy, thick materials.

c. Process principles. In the GTAW process, the tungsten alloy electrode is mounted in a special electrode holder designed to furnish a flow of inert gas around the electrode and the arc. The arc is

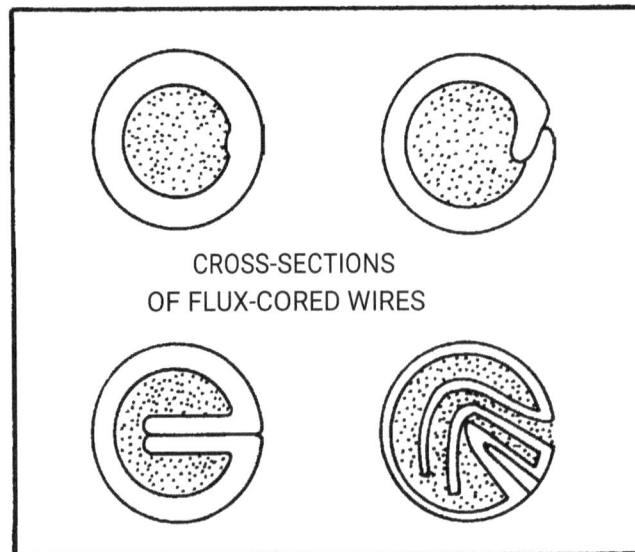

CROSS-SECTIONS
OF FLUX-CORED WIRES

Reprinted from MIL HDBK 5E, Materials and Material Processes Series -- Arc Welding, Department of Defense, 1968 (noncopyrighted).

Figure 3-21. Cross sections of flux-cored wires

struck between the base metal and the electrode by one of two methods. In the first, called a scratch start, the operator actually touches the work piece with the tungsten and withdraws slightly. The second method uses high-frequency discharge from the electrode to the work piece to establish the arc. This is better for welds that have to be very clean; a scratch start could leave particles of tungsten in the weld, causing brittle spots. After the arc is started, the filler metal, if required, is fed into the weld pool near the arc, as shown in figure 3-22. The molten weld metal, the adjacent base metal, and the electrodes are protected by a flowing gaseous envelope of inert gas: generally argon, helium, or a mixture of the two. Most GTAW is done manually, but for production or assembly type welds such as long butt welds, the system can be entirely automated. AC is used generally for aluminum and magnesium, while DC straight polarity is used for all other metals.

d. Equipment. The equipment includes an electrical power source, electrode holder (torch), tungsten or tungsten alloy electrodes, gas flow regulating equipment, and usually a remote rheostat for off-on switching and current control (fig 3-22).

(1) There are AC and DC power units with built-in high frequency generators designed specifically for GTAW. These automatically control gas and water flow when welding begins and ends. However, power supplies without these controls can also be used.

(2) If the electrode holder (torch) is water-cooled, a supply of cooling water is needed. Electrode holders are made so that electrodes and gas nozzles can be readily changed, either for different sizes or for replacement.

(3) Mechanized GTAW equipment may include electronic devices for checking and adjusting the welding torch level, equipment for work handling, provisions for initiating the arc and controlling gas and water flow, and filler metal feed mechanisms.

3-7. Submerged arc (SAW)

In the SAW process, the arc is not visible, but is submerged under a layer of granulated flux (fig 3-23). This process can be used with either a single electrode wire or many. AWS D1.1 describes the procedure, equipment, electrodes, and flux used with SAW.

a. Advantages. SAW is an efficient process that can be used on nearly all ferrous metals. Welds of very good quality are produced in a wide range of metals thicker than 1/1 6 inch. Carbon, alloy, or stainless steels up to 1/2-inch thick are welded in one pass,   while thicker materials require more passes.   Weld metal deposition rates, arc travel

speeds, and weld completion rates are better than those for other processes. There is no visible arc and no weld spatter, and the deep penetrating effect of concentrated heat allows narrow welding grooves. Thus, it takes less filler metal to make a joint with SAW than with other welding processes, The unfused flux can be recovered and recycled when the welding is finished.

b. Disadvantages. The basic limitation of SAW is that it can only be used in the flat position and for horizontal fillet welds. Welds can be made in the horizontal position,   but since the granular flux needed to shield the weld metal must be in place in front of the electrode, complicated dams and supports may be required to contain the flux. The equipment used in this process can be hand-held, but is usually mechanized, making it heavy and cumbersome and thereby limiting its use to fabrication shops. The fused flux must be removed by chipping and wire brushing.

c. Process principles. SAW takes place beneath the flux covering without sparks, spatter, smoke, or flash. The electrode and weld pool are completely covered at all times during welding. The flux makes possible these special operating conditions, which distinguish SAW from other processes. When cold, the flux does not conduct electricity; therefore, the welder must establish a conductive path for starting the arc. This can be done by scratch starting where the electrode touches the base plate or by burying some steel wool in the flux at the starting point. In the molten state, the flux becomes highly conductive. Once the arc is started, the heat produced by the current causes the surrounding flux to become molten. This forms a conductive path, which is kept molten by the continued flow of welding current. The buried part of the flux is melted; the visible part remains unchanged in both appearance and properties, and can be reused. All currents and polarities are used, depending on the desired penetration and bead shape, Reverse polarity provides the best bead shape and penetration, while straight polarity gives higher deposition rates but less penetration. Alternating current provides penetration somewhere between the two and is preferred for multi-wire welding. The fused flux is chipped off the weld and discarded.

(1) The welding electrodes must be positioned properly. Flux is fed in front of and around the electrode by a hopper. The arc is struck and the electrodes moved along the weld. The operator watches the ammeter and voltmeter readings to control current and voltage adjustments. A variable-speed motor controls the electrode feed; a power-operated

ELECTRODE HOLDER

COOLING WATER
LINES IN AND OUT

GAS LINE

TUNGSTEN
ELECTRODE

ELECTRICAL
CONDUCTOR
WITH GAS
PASSAGES

HANDLE

POWER LEAD
ELECTRICAL CONDUCTOR

GAS SHIELD CUP

INSULATING SHEATH

SHIELDING GAS EXITS
PAST ELECTRODE

FILLER ROD

GROUND CONNECTION
ATTACHED TO WORK

WELDING
MACHINE

GAS
SUPPLY

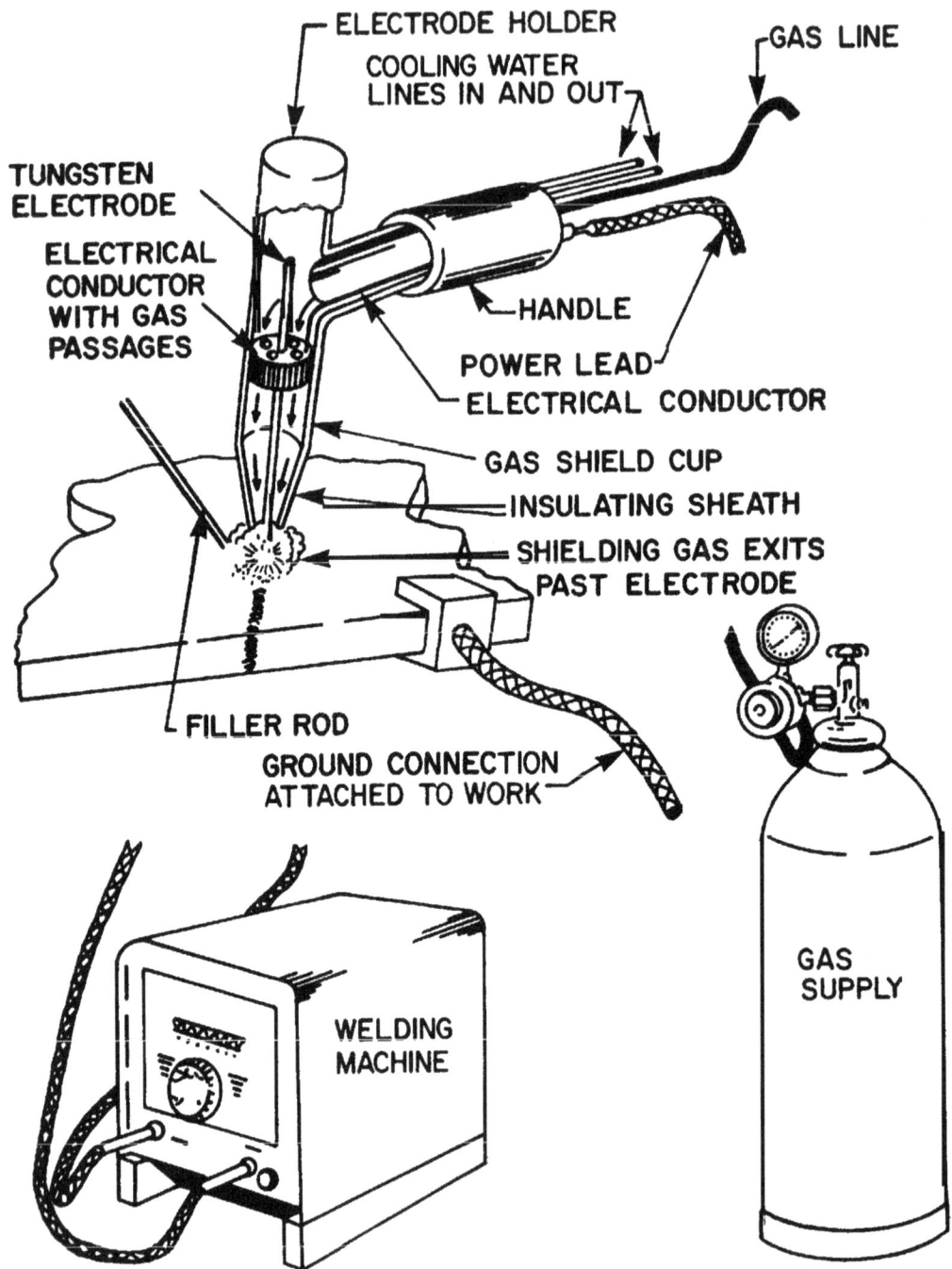

Reprinted from MIL HDBK 723A, Steel and
Wrought Products, Department of Defense,
1970 (noncopyrighted).

Figure 3-22. The GTAW process.

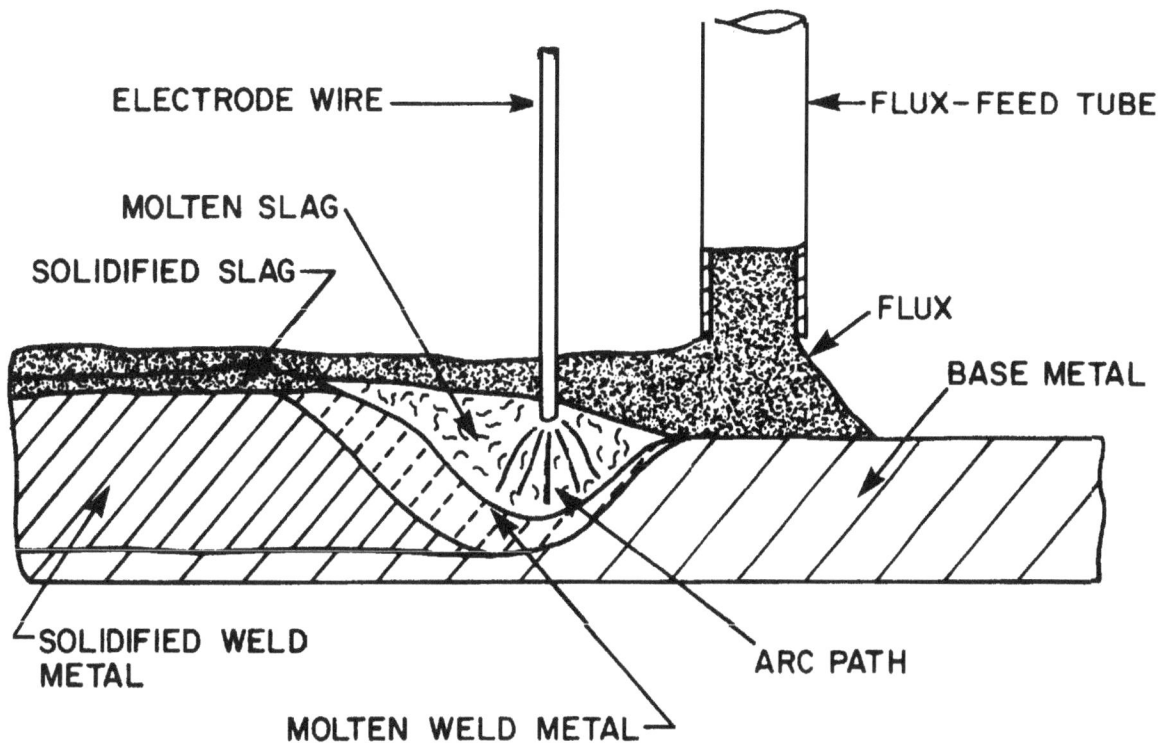

ELECTRODE WIRE →

← FLUX-FEED TUBE

MOLTEN SLAG

SOLIDIFIED SLAG

FLUX

BASE METAL

SOLIDIFIED WELD METAL

ARC PATH

MOLTEN WELD METAL

Reprinted from MIL HDBK 56, Materials and
Material Processes Series -- Arc Welding,
Department of Defense, 1968 (noncopyrighted).

Figure 3-23. The SAW process

carriage controls the travel rate. Unused flux is fed back into the hopper.

(2) Moderately thick sections of material (up to 1 inch) with a carbon content up to 0.35 percent can be welded without precautions such as preheating and postweld heat treatment. Preheating is generally needed when the carbon content is over 0.35 percent.

(3) Low-alloy steels maybe welded if the weld area is preheated to slow the rate of cooling. This must be done to avoid cracking in the weld and heat-affected zone.

(4) When certain quenched and tempered structural steels (ASTM A 514 and A 517) are welded, the heat input must be closely controlled to make sure strength and notch toughness are retained in the heat-affected zone. To keep a high level of strength and notch toughness, heat must dissipate rapidly so that desirable microstructure form. Anything that delays cooling, such as preheating or high welding heat inputs, should be avoided.

d. Equipment. Both semi-automatic and automatic SAW equipment is available; the type used generally depends on the work to be done, and on economic factors. Semi-automatic equipment is better for repair welding and for welding that cannot be done automatically because of the geometry of the part. Figure 3-24 shows the equipment needed for automatic SAW; included are a power source, wire feeding system, flux feeding system, and a welding torch.

(1) The power supply may be DC constant current, DC constant voltage, or AC. The power supply and wire-drive mechanism must be designed to operate together so that the arc length can be controlled effectively. SAW generally is done at higher currents (500 to 1000 amperes) than other types of arc welding, so the power supply must have a high current rating at high duty cycles.

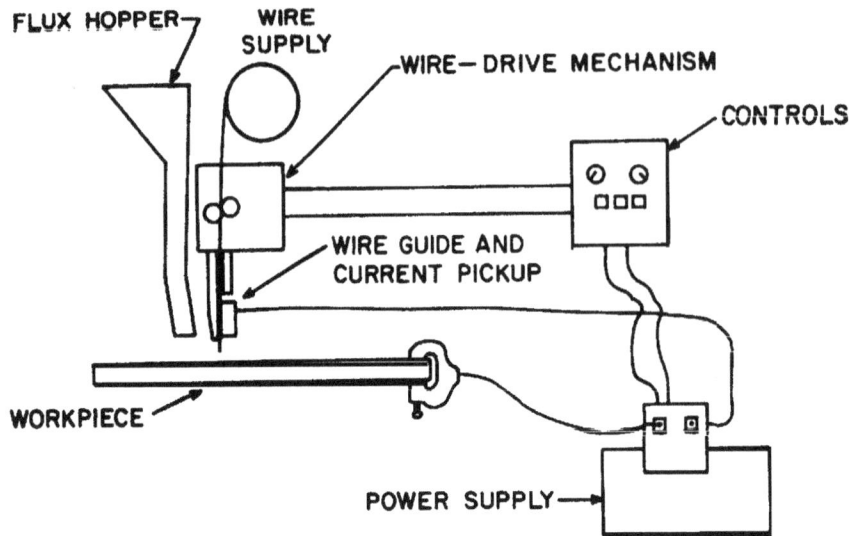

Reprinted from MIL HDBK 56, Materials and
Material Processes Series -- Arc Welding,
Department of Defense, 1968 (noncopyrighted).

Figure 3-24. Automatic SAW equipment and controls for automatic welding in the flat position.

(2) The electrodes used with SAW are generally bare rods or wire in coils. The choice of electrode depends on the way the alloying elements are introduced into the weld. One method is to use mild-steel electrodes with fluxes containing the alloy. Another method often used requires special alloy steel electrodes and neutral flux, and includes low-carbon steel, low-carbon alloy steel, special alloy steels, high-carbon steels, stainless steels, and nonferrous alloys.

(3) The fluxes are granulated, fusible mineral materials of various compositions and particle sizes. The choice of flux depends on the welding procedure, joint configuration, and composition of the base metal to be welded. The flux may include alloying elements.

3-8. Exothermic welding

In exothermic welding, heat is generated by the chemical reaction between a combination of aluminum and iron oxide. This mixture is placed in a hopper above a mold which surrounds the joint, and is then ignited. A chemical reaction occurs, and the molten metal and slag drop through the hopper. Since the molten metal is heavier than the slag, it settles to the bottom of the mold and touches the steel joint. The molten metal melts the surface of the metal and fuses with it, forming the weld. This process, commonly referred to as "thermit welding, " is used for joining reinforcing rods, rails, large castings or forgings, and for repairing large structural shapes. Historically, thermit welding was largely confined to structures made of iron and steel. But recently, the substitution of a copper oxide for iron oxide has led to many applications within the electrical industry

such as joining or repairing electrical connectors, cables, bus bars, and bus tubes. Thermit welding is also used for welding pipe. In this application the thermit does not mix with the pipe metal, but merely furnishes the heat to melt the pipe ends, which are then butted together as they melt.

a. Advantages.

(1) The welder needs very little instruction or experience to produce good welds rapidly.

(2) Large sections may be fusion welded, and large quantities of filler metal may be deposited quickly. Thermit welding can be roughly compared to a foundry casting operation. The one difference is that the metal being poured is considerably hotter than when melted in a furnace. The completed weld left in the mold cools slowly, reducing residual stress.

b. Disadvantages. Molds are needed to hold the molten metal around the weld joint. For one-of-a-kind jobs, such as repairs, the molds must be constructed individually, and a suitable wax or plastic form filler materials must be inserted in the gap to insure proper clearance between the parts. Preformed permanent molds are used for repetitive jobs — welding rails or reinforcing rods, for example.

c. Process principles. Thermit welding is based on the fundamental principle that aluminum is more chemically active than iron. The welding process consists of mixing the iron oxide and aluminum, both in powder form, and placing them in a hopper or crucible above a mold which surrounds the joint area. (The joint to be welded must be cleaned, properly spaced, and preheated.) An ignition powder, such as a mixture of barium peroxide and aluminum powder, is placed on top of the thermit, and a fuse is inserted into the powder. The reaction starts after the fuse ignites the mixture; this happens at about 2000 "F. The reaction is nonexplosive and takes about 30 seconds; once the mixture starts to burn, it is self-propagating. When the reaction is complete, the molten metal has reached a temperature of approximately 4500 °F, which is nearly 1600°F higher than the temperature of ordinary molten steel. The metal is poured into the mold to form the weld (fig 3-25). The mold is allowed to remain in position for several hours to permit solidification and to anneal the weld. The deposited metal cools uniformly and is comparatively free from stresses. The mold is then removed and the gates and risers are cut away, Excess weld can be ground or machined. Although the principal application of thermit welding has been with the aluminum and iron oxide mixture on steel structures, other metals or their oxides may be included in the thermit mixture. Chromium, nickel, manganese, tungsten, titanium, molybdenum, and cobalt can be used. These

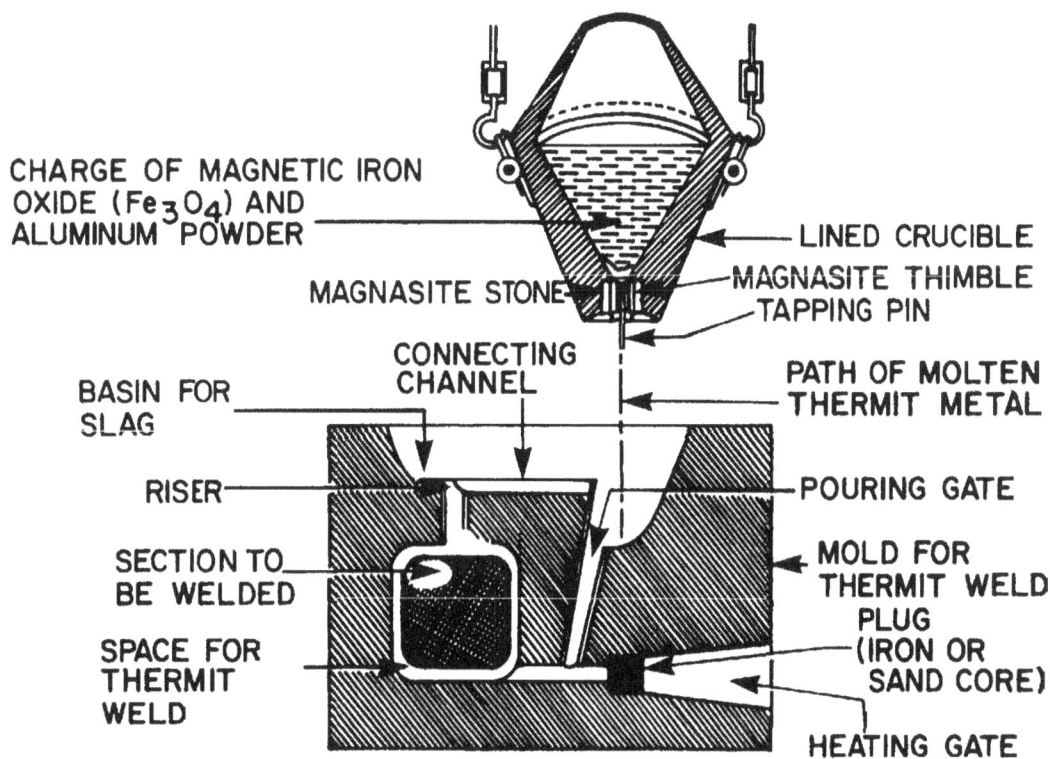

CHARGE OF MAGNETIC IRON OXIDE (Fe_3O_4) AND ALUMINUM POWDER — LINED CRUCIBLE — MAGNASITE THIMBLE — TAPPING PIN — MAGNASITE STONE — PATH OF MOLTEN THERMIT METAL — BASIN FOR SLAG — CONNECTING CHANNEL — RISER — POURING GATE — SECTION TO BE WELDED — MOLD FOR THERMIT WELD — PLUG (IRON OR SAND CORE) — SPACE FOR THERMIT WELD — HEATING GATE

Figure 3-25. Thermit welding crucible and mold.

elements alloy with iron and are used when higher strength, ductility, or hardness is required. They also permit control of the temperature and time of the reaction. Cast iron can be welded with a special thermit mixture.

d. Equipment. Thermit welding kits are available. They consist of a permanent mold, prepackaged thermit charges, consumable tapping discs, charges of ignition powder, and fuses. An individually constructed mold requires wax or foam filler, sand mold (a special mixture of silica sand and plastic clay), and gates, risers, pouring gates, and a slag basin (fig 3-25).

3-9. Arc-stud welding

Arc-stud welding is an arc welding process in which an electric arc is struck between a metal stud and another piece of metal. When the surfaces to be jointed are properly heated, they are brought together under pressure. A ceramic ferrule surrounding the stud can provide partial shielding. The process is generally referred to as "stud welding." AWS D1.1 describes stud welding procedures, equipment, workmanship, quality control, and inspection requirements.

a. Advantages. Arc-stud welding has many advantages and uses. With this process, there is no need to drill or punch holes, nor to fasten an object mechanically to a main structure with bolts, rivets, or screws. Arc-stud welding is widely accepted by all the metal-working industries. Since virtually every phase of the operation is automatic, no previous welding experience is necessary. Inexperienced operators can be trained quickly, and once the equipment is set for a particular job, high-quality welds are quickly and easily made. The welding gun

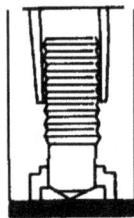

a. Gun properly positioned for stud welding

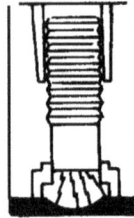

b. Trigger is depressed and stud is lifted, creating arc

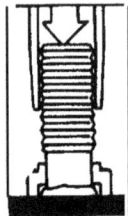

c. Arcing period is completed and stud is plunged into molten pool of metal on base plate.

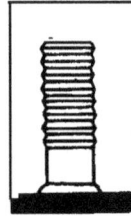

d. Gun is withdrawn from stud and ferrule is removed.

Reprinted from MIL HDBK 56, Materials and Material Processes Series -- Arc Welding, Department of Defense, 1968 (noncopyrighted).

Figure 3-26. Steps in stud welding operation

PRESSURE MANUALLY APPLIED

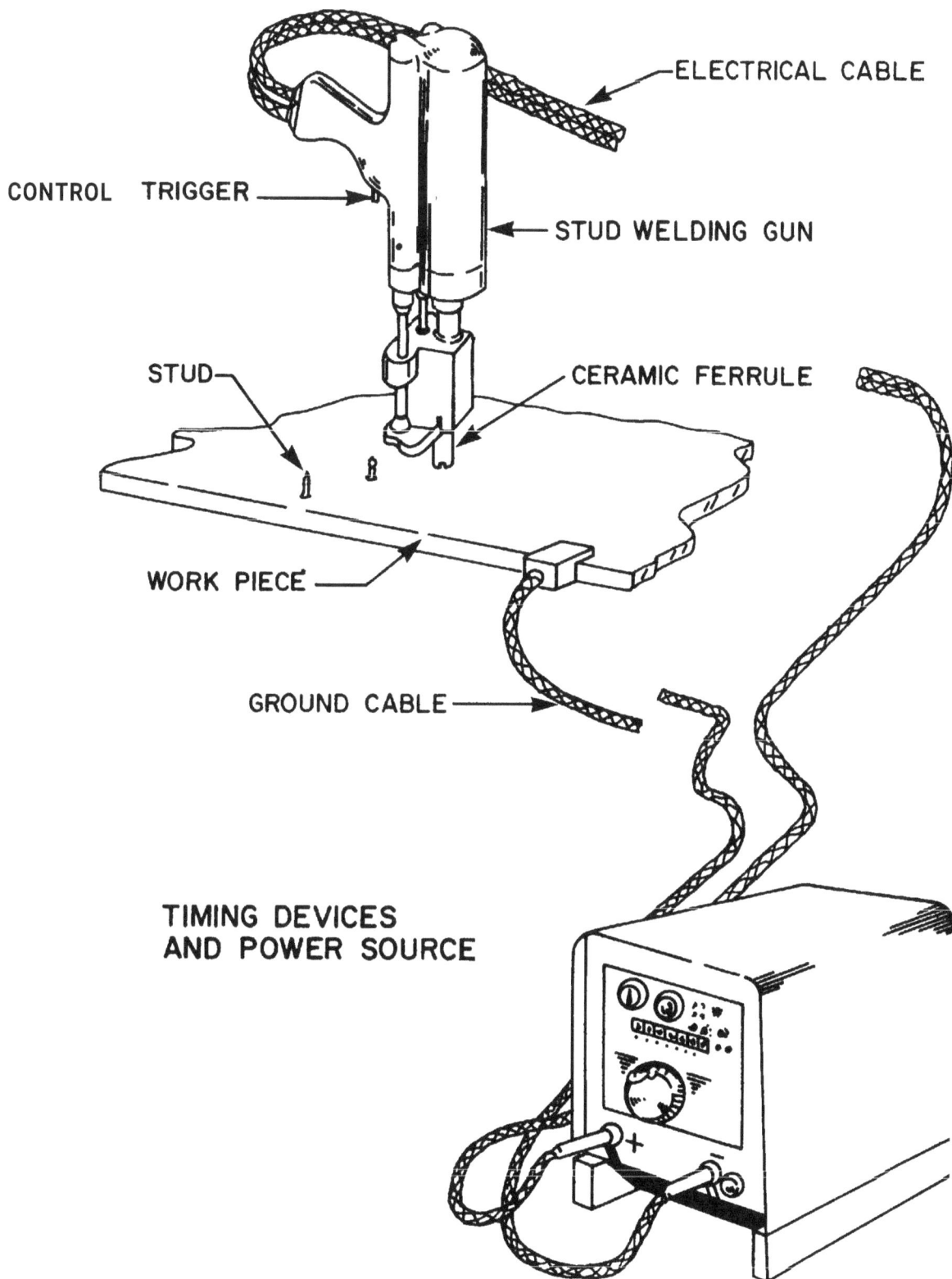

ELECTRICAL CABLE

CONTROL TRIGGER

STUD WELDING GUN

STUD

CERAMIC FERRULE

WORK PIECE

GROUND CABLE

TIMING DEVICES AND POWER SOURCE

+

−

Figure 3-27. Stud welding equipment.

is light and easy to handle, making the equipment very portable.

b. **Disadvantages.** Since this is a versatile process, there are no real disadvantages; however, there are some limitations on its use. Stud welding is approved for use on low-pressure heating boilers built under the ASME Boiler and Pressure Vessel Code for all applications except stay bolts. This includes cover plates, clean-out or access doors, and studded openings for boiler-tubing water-heater coils. Stud welding is approved for use on nonpressure parts on power boilers and unfired vessels.

c. Process principles. In the arc-stud welding process, the flux-coated stud is inserted into a collet or chuck which is an integral part of the gun. A porcelain ferrule surrounds each stud to shield the arc, hold the molten pool in place, and help form an acceptable fillet shape. The flux on the end of the stud helps the operator control the arc and make stud welds in any position. The operator places the gun in the proper position, and spring pressure from the gun holds the stud against the work piece. When the trigger is depressed, it completes an electric circuit, causing the collet to withdraw the stud from the work piece a preset distance, creating a gap and an electric arc. At the end of an automatically timed interval, the molten end of the stud is plunged into the molten pool which has formed on the surface of the plate. The process is similar to conventional metallic-arc welding because, in effect, the stud serves as a consumable electrode while the current is flowing. The molten metal quickly solidifies and the collet releases the stud (fig 3-26). The operator removes the gun and is ready for the next welding operation, all within seconds. Stainless steel, magnesium, and aluminum can be welded with basically the same equipment as that used for steel — except inert gas must be fed through the gun to protect the weld.

(1) In practice, the same restrictions apply both to the metal-arc welding of carbon steels and to stud welding. Carbon steels with a carbon content up to 0.30 percent may be welded without preheating. When the carbon content exceeds 0.30 percent, particularly in heavy sections, preheating is advisable to prevent cracking in the heat-affected zone. In some cases, a combination of preheating and postheating has proven helpful.

(2) Low-alloy steels may be satisfactorily stud welded without preheating if the carbon content is held to 0.15 percent maximum. To prevent cracking in the heat-affected zone, preheating is necessary when the carbon content exceeds 0.15 percent.

(3) The heat-treatable, high-strength, low-alloy structural steels require more attention since they usually are hardenable enough to form martensite in the heat-affected zone. These steels are quite sensitive to underbead cracking, and the weld area is usually low in ductility. Preheating to about 700°F is recommended when steels of this category are stud welded.

d. Equipment. The equipment for stud welding consists of a DC power source; stud welding gun; welding cables; ferrules for shielding the arc; and controls, including timing devices. The equipment is usually portable, but stationary equipment for large-scale operations is used widely.

(1) The power source is a normal welding machine adapted for stud welding. The cables are made the same way as standard welding cables. The gun is designed to assure correct alignment and hold the stud. This gun has a trigger to start current flow and a timing device that withdraws the stud at the proper time to create the arc, moves the stud into the molten pool, and holds it until the molten pool solidifies (fig 3-27).

(2) A ferrule is used with each stud. It shields the arc, protects the welder, and eliminates the need for a full face helmet. The ferrule concentrates heat during welding and confines molten metal to the weld area. It helps prevent both oxidation of the molten metal during the arcing cycle and charring of the work piece.

(3) Studs are available in a variety of shapes, sizes, and diameters. Some are designed for threading or riveting, others serve as nails. Studs are available as straight and bent shapes, hooks, or eyebolts.

3-10. Process selection

Table 3-2 is a selection guide for the welding processes discussed in this chapter. This table is based on the particular applications encountered in field welding.

Table 3-2. Summary of welding processes and application

Conditions	SHAW	GMAW Free Flight	GMAW Pulsed Current	GMAW Short Current	Flux-Cored	Arc GTAW	SAW	Exothermic	Stud
Materials commonly welded	Steel, cast iron, wrought iron, nickel, nickel alloys, stainless steel	All except brass, cast iron, wrought iron, lead, tungsten			Steel	All	Steel and stainless steel	Steel, cast iron, electrical, copper	Steel, titanium, aluminum
Normal use	Manual	Semi. & auto.°	Semi. & auto.	Semi. & auto.	Semi.& auto.	Manual & auto.	Semi. & auto.	Manual	
Welding position	All	Flat & horizontal fillets°°	All	All	All	All	Flat & horizontal fillets	Flat	All
Base Metal thickness	All	1/4 inch & up	All	All	1/4 inch & up	All	1/4 inch & up	All	All

° Note: Semi = semi-automatic; auto = automatic
°° Welding positions = flat, horizontal, vertical, and overhead

CHAPTER 4

WELDING OF STAINLESS STEEL

4-1. General

Stainless steels were originally developed because of their outstanding resistance to corrosion. They also exhibit good mechanical properties, which can be as important to the life of the structure as the corrosion resistance. There are four types of stainless steel: martensitic, ferritic, austenitic, and precipitation hardened. These steels exhibit a wide range of mechanical properties both at room temperatures and at cryogenic temperatures (below – 150 degrees F). The stainless steels commonly used are covered in specifications of ASTM, the American Iron and Steel Institute (AISI), the Society of Automotive Engineers (SAE), ASME, API, and the military or other Federal agencies. Commonly used stainless steels are the austenitic class that meet specifications for AISI grades in the 200 and 300 series. Martensitic stainless steels in the AISI 400 series are also used. When designing for 400 series stainless steels, one must use extra care because of their sensitivity in heat treating. Stainless steels that conform to other specifications can be used where particular requirements must be met. Stainless steel welding electrodes are specified by AWS or military documents. Commonly used welding electrodes for fabrication meet specifications AWS A5.4, A5.9, A5.11, A5.14, and A5.22.

4-2. Weldability of stainless steels

The austenitic chromium-nickel steels are often used for cryogenic and vacuum systems. These steels are characterized by their corrosion resistance, low-magnetic permeability, good high-temperature strength, and excellent low-temperature ductility and notch toughness. Some of the austenitic steels, however, do have characteristics that restrict their use in cryogenic applications (table 4-1). But the austenitic steels are considered the most weldable of the high alloy steels. Three basic factors affect the weldability of stainless steels: (1) the chemical composition of the base metal and the weld metal, (2) the microstructure of the base metal and the weld metal, and (3) the use of the correct welding procedures and techniques

a. Chemical composition. The major constituents in stainless steels are iron , carbon, manganese, silicon, chromium, and nickel. The chromium is primarily responsible for the stain and corrosion resistance of these steels. It has an affinity for oxygen and forms a thin, impervious, protective, oxide layer. Chromium also has an affinity for carbon and forms chromium-carbides rapidly between 800 and 1600°F.

(1) When chromium-carbides are formed, they tie up much of the chromium and severely reduce the corrosion resistance of the steel. Typically, this can happen in a zone next to and on either side of the weld joint. This phenomenon, known as sensitization, occurs because a region next to the weld is heated to between 800 and 1600 "F by the welding arc. If the weld joint is subjected to a corrosive environment, knife-line attack results. Three techniques are used to mitigate sensitization. These methods can be expensive and should be used only when sensitization is a problem.

(a) Extra-low carbon (less than 0.03 percent carbon) grades of steel can be used. This carbon content is the maximum amount that is soluble in stainless steels and does not easily come out of solution.

(b) Stabilizing elements such as columbium and tantalum can be used. These form carbides preferentially over chromium, thereby tying up the carbon.

(c) A post-weld heat treatment can be used. The most common heat treatment technique is to solution anneal at 1900°F, then water quench. This technique puts all the carbon in solution and keeps it there by rapidly cooling through the 1600 to 800 °F range.

(2) In a fully austenitic stainless steel weld (such as a type 310), the ductility and soundness of the weld depend on the carbon to silicon ratio. Ideally, this ratio should be about 1:2. An increase in silicon above this ratio causes fissuring (microcracking) in the weld metal and a rapid loss of ductility. An increase in the carbon ratio causes a less severe decrease in ductility without affecting weld soundness. With fully austenitic stainless steels, the carbon to silicon ratio must be closely controlled. This tends to limit the use of such steels when weld joints with the best quality and ductility are required.

b. Microstructural effects. Two microstructural factors affect the quality of austenitic stainless steel weld joints: ferrite content in weld metal and base metal, and grain growth in weld metal and the heat-affected zone. The following discussion describes methods of controlling these factors. Designers can use this information to specify the proper base materials, and welding procedures and materials.

(1) Ferrite content.

(a) Fully austenitic weld joints often tend to develop microcracks and fissures during welding. To prevent this, designers should select filler metals or electrodes that will form an austenitic weld deposit containing a small percentage of ferrite. Such welds are highly resistant to cracking. However, if the ferrite content becomes too high in cryogenic applications, the weld metal's impact strength at service temperatures can be seriously reduced. For these applications. the ferrite content of the weld metal should be within the range of 4 to 10 percent.

(b) The actual ferrite content depends on the compositions of the base metal and filler metal or electrode, and the extent to which the weld metal deposit is diluted by the welded parent metal. A Schaeffler diagram (fig 4-1) can help designers estimate both the percentage of ferrite in the weld deposit and the filler metal composition necessary to form the required ferrite in the weld metal. This diagram is used to predict the amount of ferrite in stainless steel weld metal on the basis of weld metal composition.   The diagram shows how the microstructure of the weld deposit is affected by the alloy elements in stainless steel that act like nickel, and those that act like chromium. The nickel equivalent group which is the austenite former includes nickel, carbon, and manganese; an allowance is also made for the nitrogen content. The chromium equivalent group which is the ferrite former includes chromium, molybdenum, silicon, and columbium. The nickel equivalent is the ordinate of the diagram, and the chromium is the abscissa.

(c) To estimate the microstructure of the weld metal, the designer uses the following formulas to calculate the nickel and chromium equivalents:

nickel equivalent   = % nickel + 30 X % carbon + 0.5 X % manganese

chromium equivalent =   70 chromium + % molybdenum + 1.5 X % silicon + 0.5 X % columbium.

The nickel and chromium equivalents are calculated for both the base and weld metal. The values obtained are then plotted on the Schaeffler diagram, and a line is drawn between the two points to indicate the possible ferrite percentages that could be in

the weld metal because of base metal dilution. For example, if type 302 stainless steel is welded using type 308 electrode, then the nickel equivalent for the 302 stainless is 12, and the chromium equivalent is 18.25. When this point is plotted, it is totally in the austenitic region, so there will be no ferrite. The type 308 electrode will have a nickel equivalent of 12, and a chromium equivalent of 21, thus putting it close to the 10 percent ferrite line.

(d) The Schaeffler diagram can predict not only the amount of ferrite in the microstructure, but also the electrode composition that will prevent excessive ferrite or martensite content in stainless steel weld metal. In addition, the diagram is helpful in estimating the trend of the microstructure developed when dissimilar steels are welded. If pieces of carbon steel and stainless steel are to be welded together, the compositions of the two can be marked on the diagram; the tie line drawn between them indicates   the microstructure   that may be encountered.

(2) Grain growth. The toughness and ductility of the heat-affected zone and the weld metal may be reduced somewhat because of grain growth caused by the welding heat. However, unless extremely high welding heats are used or very heavy weld passes are deposited, the problem of decreased toughness and ductility resulting from grain growth is not serious. If impact testing of sample weld joints indicates that the notch toughness of the weld metal or heat-affected zone has suffered, the welding process should be modified to decrease the heat input to the joint and thus restrict the amount of grain growth.

c. Preweld and postweld heat treating. Weld joints in stainless steel are neither preheated nor postheated. These techniques make the joints cool slowly and could cause sensitization, with a resulting loss of notch toughness. However, rapid cooling after welding prevents sensitization of the weld metal and heat-affected zone. In multipass welds, the maximum interpass temperature should be 300 "F. Stress relieving of austenitic stainless steel weld joints also should be avoided because it seldom works and sensitization can occur easily.

d. Weld cracking.

(1) Weld cracking in austenitic stainless steels can be divided into four types: crater cracks, star cracks, hot cracks or microfissures, and root cracks. All four types of cracking are believed to be manifestations of the same basic kind of cracking — namely hot cracking, or in its earliest stage, microfissuring.   Hot cracking presented many difficulties some years ago, but now it can be prevented in

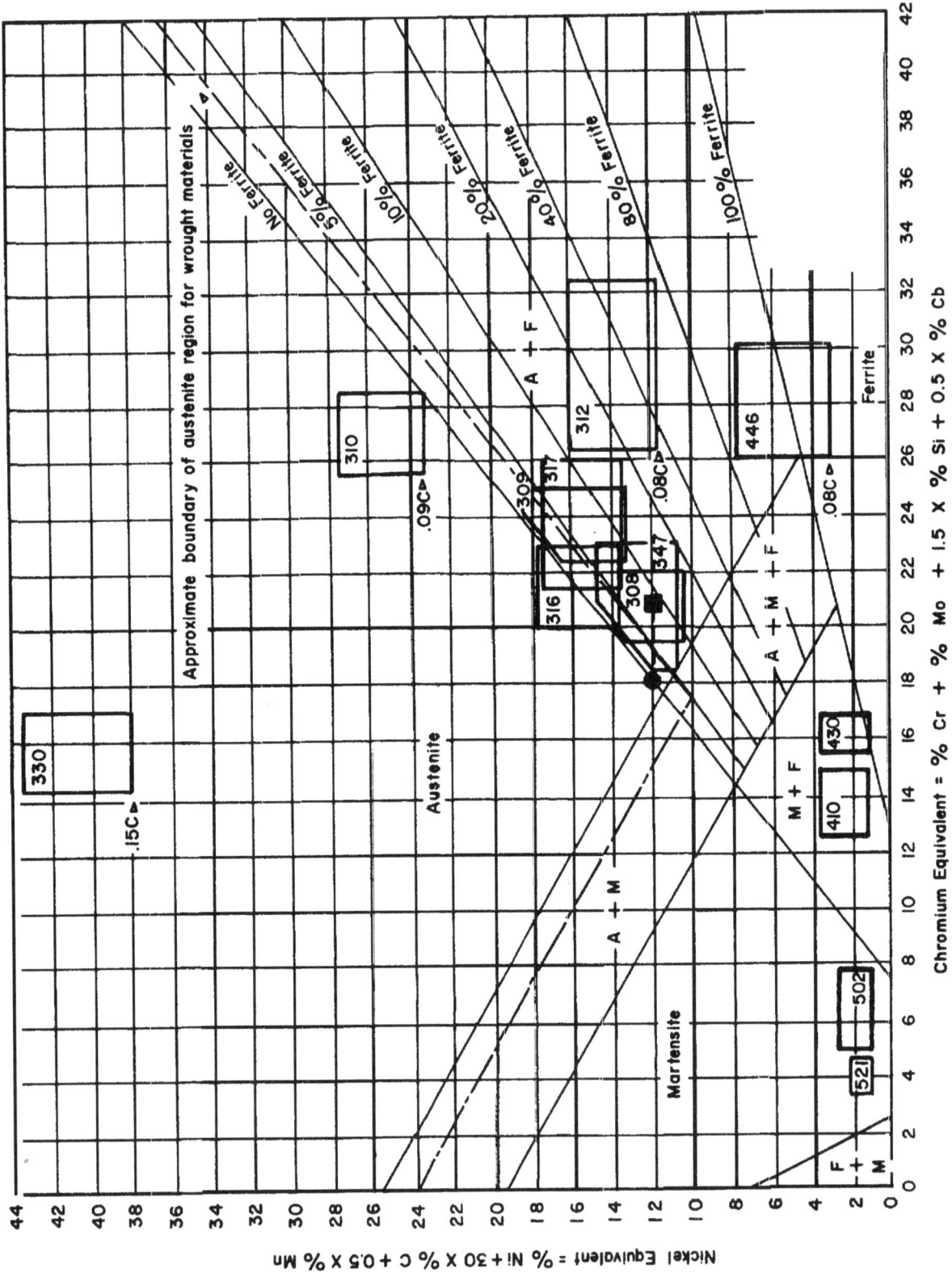

Figure 4-1. Schaeffler's diagram for the microstructure of stainless steel welds.

Reprinted from TM 5-805-7. Welding Design, Procedures and Inspection, Department of the Army, 1968 (noncopyrighted).

weldments. Hot cracks occur intergranularly; apparently, the segregation of low melting constituents in the grain boundaries induces fissuring susceptibility.

(a) The formation of microfissures seems to depend on five factors: the microstructure of the weld metal; the composition of the weld metal, particularly the level of residual elements; the amount of stress imposed on the weld as it cools through the high temperature range; the ductility of the weld metal at high temperatures; and the presence of notches that form incipient cracks at the edge of the weld.

(b) For many years, it was believed that microfissures only developed in the as-deposited weld metal shortly after solidification. However, more recent work has clearly shown that microfissures can occur in the heat-affected zones of previously deposited sound weld beads.

(2) The microstructure of the weld metal strongly affects microfissuring susceptibility. Weld metal having a wholly austenitic micro-structure is a lot more sensitive to conditions that promote microfissuring than weld metal containing some delta or free ferrite in the austenitic matrix. As discussed in a above, the chemical composition —— both alloy content and residual element content — strongly influences rnicrofissuring susceptibility of the wholly austenitic stainless steel weld metals. Microfissuring is reduced by a small increase in carbon content, a substantial increase in manganese, or an increase in the nitrogen content. The residual elements that influence cracking most often are boron, phosphorus, sulfur, selenium, silicon, columbium, and tantalum.

(3) In welding austenitic stainless steels, two different practices are now used, depending on the microstructure expected in the weld metal.

(a) Whenever possible, ferrite-containing austenitic weld structure is used. The filler metal must be selected carefully and the welding procedure planned in detail to secure the small, but important, amount of delta ferrite. The Schaeffler diagram, discussed in b above, has been used frequently for determining whether a specified weld composition will contain enough ferrite.

(b) When a wholly austenitic weld structure must be used, welding materials containing the lowest possible amount of recognized crack promoters should be selected. In addition, the amount of alloy elements known to improve crack resistance should be increased. Even with the best materials and the most favorable welding procedure, wholly austenitic deposits are more crack sensitive than the ferrite-containing types. Therefore, all phases of welding and inspection need greater care.

(4) Base metal heat-affected zone cracking in welded austenitic stainless steels can be a problem in heavier sections (more than 1-inch thick). Such cracking can have two causes. One is an intergranular form of hot shortness in a heat-affected zone during welding. The weld metal cracks because of grain boundary liquation or embrittlement at or near welding temperatures. The other cause for cracking is a complex phenomenon involving strain-induced precipitation in the heat-affected zone during post-weld heat treatments or service at high temperatures (above 450 °F). A change in mechanical properties thus results in stress-rupture failure under certain conditions. In this form of failure, the key to the problem is the precipitation of columbium carbides in the stressed heat-affected zones. As little as 0.1 percent columbium as a residual element can produce strain-induced precipitation and cause welded heavy sections to fail by cracking during service at high temperatures. A titanium-stabilized stainless steel, such as type 347, can be used to help keep a nonstabilized stainless steel from cracking.

e. Other weld defects. Defects besides cracking occur in the weld metal if an incorrect weld process or technique is used. These defects include porosity, slag inclusions, incomplete fusion, inadequate joint penetration, and undercutting.

(1) Porosity is a cavity-type discontinuity formed by gas entrapped during solidification. The gases that form porosity are either driven from solution in the weld metal because of low volubility at lower temperatures, or are produced by chemical reactions in the molten weld pool. These gases are trapped in the weld metal because solidification occurs before the gases have time to rise to the surface of the pool. Porosity will form less often if very high currents or long arc lengths are avoided. The welding contractor must make sure these variables are taken into account when the procedure is developed and the welder qualification tests are conducted. This is especially true for the SMAW process because high currents and long arc lengths consume large amounts of deoxidants in the electrode covering, leaving little to combine with the excess gases in the weld pool. Moreover, the type and distribution of porosity will give some indications of its cause. The types of porosity arc classified in the acceptance standards of the various codes (ASME, API, or AWS, as applicable). Generally, the types of porosity depend on the distance between individual pores or groups of pores.

(a) Uniforrnly scattered porosity can be found in many weldments and is of little concern because there is usually enough sound metal between the pores.

(b) Clustered porosity is often associated with changes in arc conditions. For instance, areas where the arc has been started or stopped frequently contain cluster porosity.

(c) Linear porosity is usually found in the root pass and is considered a special case of inadequate joint penetration.

(2) Slag inclusions are oxides or nonmetallic solids that become trapped in solidifying metal. The inclusions either can be completely surrounded by weld metal or can be between the weld metal and the base plate. In the SMAW process, chemical reactions between the weld metal and the coating materials produce a nonmetallic slag that has low volubility in the weld metal and generally will float to the surface. Sometimes, the slag is forced into the weld metal by the stirring action of the arc, or flows ahead of the arc and is covered by the weld metal. Proper cleaning and preparation of the weld joint or proper manipulation of the electrode will reduce the number of slag inclusions. The welding contractor can make sure these precautions are included when welding procedures are developed and welder qualification tests are conducted.

(3) Incomplete fusion occurs when two weld beads, or the base metal and a weld bead, have not fused together. This is caused by failure to raise the adjoining material to the fusion temperature or failure to dissolve any oxides or other foreign material on the surface to which the new weld bead must fuse. Incomplete fusion can be prevented by following the approved welding procedure, which should include cleaning of the preceding bead and contiguous base metal in the weld joint. Particular care should be used in welding stainless steel because the high temperature increases the amount of chromium oxide formed and the steel becomes hard to weld with the increased oxide layer.

(4) Inadequate joint penetration occurs when the fusion of the weld and the base metal at the root of the joint is less than specified by design. Poor penetration affects weld joints that will be stressed in service; the root forms a notch that acts as a stress concentrator, which leads to early failure of the joint. Although a poorly cleaned joint may cause inadequate penetration, poor heat transfer conditions in the joint are more often at fault. Heat transfer can be increased by using wider angles for V-grooves or a larger root opening.

(5) Undercutting refers to either a sharp recess in the side wall of a weld joint or reduced thickness of the base plate at the toe of the last weld bead on the surface of the plate. In both cases, the welder's technique is the primary cause. High currents or high voltages, as well as low current and fast travel

speeds, may increase the tendency to undercut. If undercutting is a sharp recess in the joint side wall, it should be smoothed out by grinding or chipping before the next weld bead is placed. AWS specifications and the ASME Boiler and Pressure Vessel Code impose limitations on undercutting.

4-3. Joint design

Weld joints are prepared either by plasma-arc cutting or by machining or grinding, depending on the alloy. Before welding, the joint surfaces must be cleaned of all foreign material, such as paint, dirt, scale, or oxides. Cleaning may be done with suitable solvents (e. g., acetone or alcohol) or light grinding. Care should be taken to avoid nicking or gouging the joint surface since such flaws can interfere with the welding operation.

4-4. Methods of welding stainless steels

Stainless steels are readily weldable in the field by SMAW, GMAW, FCAW, and SAW processes. GTAW can be used for field fabrication, but it is a slow process. SMAW is used most often because the equipment is portable and easy to use. GMAW, FCAW, and SAW are being used more often in the field because they are economical and produce high-quality welds. Manufacturers' recommendations for welding stainless steel should be followed. These include recommendations on joint designs, preheat temperatures, any associated post-weld heat treatment, and shielding gas.

4-5. Shielded metal-arc (SMAW)

SMAW has been the preferred method of welding because of its versatility, simplicity of equipment, and wide selection of electrodes available — all of which are important for field welding applications. AWS A5.4 is the specification for stainless steel SMAW electrodes.

a. Electrode classification system. The SMAW electrode classification code contains an E and three numbers, followed by a dash and either a 15 or 16 (EXXX-15). The E designates that the material is an electrode, and the three digits indicate composition. Sometimes there are letters following the three digits; these letters indicate a modification of the standard composition. The 15 or 16 specify the type of current with which these electrodes may be used. Both designations indicate that the electrode is usable in all positions: flat, horizontal, overhead, and vertical.

(1) The 15 indicates that the covering of this electrode is a lime type, which contains a large proportion of calcium or alkaline earth materials; these electrodes are usable with DC reverse-polarity only.

(2) The designation 16 indicates electrodes that have a lime- or titania-type covering with a large proportion of titanium-bearing minerals. The coverings of these electrodes also contain readily ionizing elements — such as potassium — to stabilize the arc for AC welding.

b. Chemical requirements. The SMAW electrode requirements for the nickel-chromium austenitic stainless steels are included in AWS A5.4. The chemical requirements are based on the as-deposited weld metal chemistry. Chemical requirements do not change when a 15 or 16 electrode is used.

c. Weld metal mechanical properties. The AWS requires the deposited weld metal to have a minimum tensile strength of 60,000 to 100,000 psi, with minimum elongations of 20 to 35 percent. The detailed requirements are in AWS A5.4.

d. Recommended filler metals for austenitic stainless steels. The *Welding Handbook,* section 4, "Metals and Their Weldability, " chapter 64, "The 4-10 Percent Chromium-Molybdenum Steels and the Straight Chromium Stainless Steels, " has a table giving a complete list of base metals by AISI number and recommended filler metals to join the base metals. This table lists not only the chromium stainless steels, but also heat-resisting stainless steels and all the austenitic stainless steels. If the type of stainless steel is not listed, then manufacturers' recommendations should be followed. An appendix to AWS A5.4 describes the intended uses of the electrodes.

4-6. Gas metal-arc (GMAW)

GMAW is being used more often for shop and field Applications because it offers much less downtime for electrode changes, less loss resulting from stub ends and spatter, and minimal interpass cleaning compared to the SMAW process. GMAW can be done in all positions by using either short-circuiting transfer or a pulsed voltage power supply. GMAW has slightly less versatility than SMAW because the welding gun is bulkier than the electrode holder for the SMAW; furthermore, the equipment is more complex and expensive, and requires somewhat more skill by the operator,

a. Electrode classification system. The classification code for GMAW electrode wire consists of an E, an R, and three digits: ERXXX. The letter E indicates that this is an electrode material, and the R indicates that it is a welding rod. Since these filler metals are used for the atomic hydrogen and GTAW method as well as for SAW and GMAW, both letters are used. The three-digit number, such as 308 in ER308, designates the chemical composition of the filler metal. An "Si" after the classification indicates

that the rod or electrode contains between 0.5 and 1 percent silicon rather than the standard 0.25 to 0.60 percent silicon. An "L" indicates that this electrode has a carbon content not exceeding 0.03 percent. The specifications for these electrodes are contained in AWS A5.9.

b. Chemical requirements. The chemical requirements for the GMAW electrodes are in AWS A5.9. The proportions of elements are similar in electrodes and base metal with the same designation. All chemical analyses are based on the as-manufactured electrode wire.

c. Weld metal mechanical properties. The all-weld metal tensile properties for the chromium-nickel austenitic stainless steel electrodes are presented in the appendix of AWS A5.9. These mechanical properties are the same as those required for the SMAW electrodes.

d. Shielding gas. Two types of shield gas are used with the GMAW process: pure argon and argon plus 2 percent oxygen. The minimum thickness which can be welded using this process is about 1/8 to 3/16 inch.

e. Recommended filler metals for chromium-nickel stainless steels. The austenitic stainless steels are listed by AISI specification numbers in the table "Covered Electrodes Recommended for Welds Between Stainless and Heat-Resisting Steels" in the *Welding Handbook,* section 4, chapter 64. If steels other than those listed are used, then the manufacturer's recommendation for weld metals and preheat temperatures should be followed. An appendix to AWS A5.9 describes the intended uses of the electrode types.

4-7, Flux-cored arc welding (FCAW)

FCAW uses equipment similar to that of GMAW, and offers the advantages of high deposition and fluxing ingredients. This process is used primarily in the flat and horizontal positions, but can be used in other positions if the proper electrode diameter and welding currents are selected. Flux-cored, corrosion-resisting chromium and chromium-nickel steel electrodes are specified by AWS A5.22.

a. Electrode classification system. The FCAW electrodes are classified similarly to the GMAW electrodes. In the code EXXXT-Y, the EXXX designation is the same as for the GMAW electrodes and can be any of the material classification numbers previously noted. The letter T indicates a continuous tubular electrode with a powdered flux within the tube. The suffix Y can be any number from 1 to 3 or the letter G. The numbers indicate the external shielding medium to be used during welding. A " 1" designates an electrode using carbon dioxide shielding gas. A "2" designates an electrode using a mixture of argon plus 2 percent oxygen. A "3" designates an electrode using no external shielding gas because the shielding is provided by the core material. The "G" indicates an electrode with an unspecified method of shielding; no requirements are imposed on it.

b. Chemical requirements. A table in AWS A5.22 presents the deposited weld metal's chemical analysis for austenitic chromium-nickel stainless steel FCAW electrodes. All classifications of the FCAW electrodes have chemical requirements except the G classification, and those requirements are only as agreed on between the supplier and the purchaser.

c. Weld metal mechanical properties. The all-weld metal tensile requirements for the austenitic chromium-nickel stainless steel FCAW electrodes are presented in a table in AWS A5.22. The tensile strength minimums vary from 60,000 to 80,000 psi, with a minimum elongation between 20 and 35 percent. The G classification of the electrodes does not have any requirements except those the supplier and purchaser agree on.

d. Shielding gas. The FCAW electrodes can use three types of shielding: carbon dioxide, argon plus 2 percent oxygen, or inner shield. The inner shield method uses gas-producing materials within the core of the electrode. The shielding gas for the G designation electrode is not specified.

e. Recommended filler metals for austenitic chromium-nickel stainless steels. The recommended filler metal/base metal combinations for the AISI-designated stainless steels are in a table in the *Welding Handbook,* section 4, chapter 64. If stainless steels other than those listed are to be used, then manufacturers' recommendations for weld metal should be followed. An appendix to AWS A5.22 for FCAW electrodes lists the intended uses of the electrodes.

4-8. Submerged arc (SAW)

The SAW process is limited to flat position and horizontal fillet welds because a granulated flux is used to protect the arc and the molten weld metal. SAW electrodes are specified by AWS A5.9. This is the same specification for the GMAW electrodes. For SAW, DC reverse polarity or AC may be used. Basic fluxes are generally recommended to minimize silicon pickup and the oxidation of chromium and other elements. In general, electrodes having a silicon content of 0.6 percent or less are desirable for submerged arc welding since the fluxes usually

result in some silicon pickup. The material classification, chemical requirements, and mechanical property requirements are the same as those for the GMAW electrodes in the as-welded condition. The recommended filler metals for the austenitic chromium-nickel stainless steel are the same as those for the GMAW electrode and are listed in the table in the *Welding Handbook,* section 4, chapter 64, as noted in the above discussion of the recommended filler metals for other processes.

4-9. Special considerations in welding stainless steels

a. Effects of thermal properties of stainless steel on welding conditions and distortion. The thermal properties (coefficients of thermal conductivity and expansion, and melting point) of stainless steel differ somewhat from those of carbon steels. The differences affect the welding operations, and steps must be taken to compensate for the effects of these thermal properties. These steps are discussed in paragraph 7-5.

b. Welding characteristics.

(1) Generally, austenitic stainless steel can be welded with about 20 percent less heat input than carbon steels. There are several reasons for this. Stainless steels have a higher electrical resistivity than do carbon steels. As a result, stainless steels get hotter than carbon steels when the same welding current is used. Thus, a given amount of stainless steel can be melted with less current than the same amount of carbon steel. In addition, less heat or current is needed to melt austenitic stainless steels because they have lower melting points than carbon steel. Finally, the heat conductivity y of these stainless steels is lower than that of other steels. Therefore, the heat built up in the metal from the welding operation flows away from the weld at a slower rate. The result is that during welding, higher temperatures are reached in a shorter time.

(2) When welded, austenitic stainless steels tend to warp and buckle more than carbon steel. This is because the coefficient of thermal expansion of austenitic stainless steel is about 1-1/2 times as large as that of carbon steel. This problem is further aggravated by stainless steel's lower thermal conductivity, which tends to concentrate welding heat in a smaller area. To keep warping and buckling to a minimum, jigs and fixtures, carefully selected welding sequences, and accurate fitup generally have to be used. Preheating to reduce distortion should be avoided when welding austenitic stainless steel since this could lead to sensitization of portions of the weld joint.

(3) Special precautions are required if tack welding is used to control distortion and maintain joint alignment. If these precautions are not taken, tack welds can be a source of weldmetal cracking, porosity, incomplete penetration, or lack of fusion. A tack weld must be of the same quality as the rest of the weld. It should be inspected to ensure that it is sound and does not contain tiny cracks or porosity, The surface of the tack weld should be ground to a smooth, concave contour so that it will be completely melted into the final weld.

Table 4-1. Austenitic stainless steels most commonly used for cryogenic and uacuum environment equipment

AISI Type	Comments
201 202 301 302	Normally not used for cryogenic applications. Occasionally may be used for fittings.
304 304L	Most often used for cryogenic applications. Maintains excellent notch toughness at lowest service temperatures. Low carbon 304L less subject to sensitization.
308 308L	Contains higher Cr and Ni contents than Types 304 and 304L for better corrosion resistance. Normally not used for cryogenic applications as base metal. Most often used composition for welding electrodes and filler wires.
310	Fully austenitic and subject to cracking during welding. Sometimes used for fittings.
316 316L	Commonly used for cryogenic applications. Contains molybdenum for improved corrosion resistance. Commonly used for fittings.
321	Not used for cryogenic applications due to low notch toughness.
347	Sometimes used for cryogenic applications. Stabilized with columbium to prevent carbide precipitation

CHAPTER 5

WELDING CARBON STEEL AND LOW-ALLOY STEELS

5-1. General

The steels commonly used in constructing buildings, bridges, and piping systems are covered in specifications of ASTM, AISI, ASME, SAE, and APL These specifications often refer to the same types of steels, although they put different restrictions on the chemical analysis and mechanical properties. Commonly used materials for welded construction in buildings and bridges meet specifications ASTM A 36, A 203, A 242, A 440, A 441, A 514, A 517, A 572, or A 588; and for piping systems, specifications ASTM A 53, A 106, A 134, A 139, A 671, A 672 or A 691 or API 5L, 5LX, or 2H. Carbon or low-alloy steels which conform to any of many other specifications (including military and Federal) can be used where particular requirements must be met. Welding electrodes for steel are specified by MIL-E-22200. Commonly used welding electrodes for construction meet specifications AWS A5.1, A5.5, A5.17, A5.18, and A5.20, and A5.23.

5-2. Weldability of carbon and low-alloy steels

The AWS defines weldability as "the capacity of a metal to be welded under the fabrication conditions imposed into a specific, suitably designed structure and to perform satisfactorily in the intended service" (AWS A3.0, p. 55). Given this definition, it is clear that many things affect the weldability of a specific steel, including joint design, welding process, base metal chemistry, weld metal chemistry, mechanical properties, and impact properties. Generally, steels specified for welded building and bridge construction and for piping systems are weldable, with good mechanical properties obtained by proper attention to welding procedures and electrode selection. AWS D1.1 contains a selection guide in the Technique section that matches electrode types with various ASTM and API steels. Manufacturers' recommendations should be followed in developing welding procedures, including heat treatment and stress relief for high-strength/low-alloy steels conforming to ASTM A 514, A 517, or A 710.

a. Welding procedures The welding procedure to use is governed by the base plate, the structure being welded, the position of the weld (i.e., flat, overhead, horizontal, or vertical), and the chemical composition of the metal. Carbon levels in the base metal govern the level of preheat temperature used. As a rule, the higher the carbon level, the higher the preheat temperature used. Recommended preheat practices are given in AWS D1.1. Improper welding can introduce into the weld joint defects such as porosity, slag inclusions, incomplete fusion, inadequate joint penetration, undercutting, and cracking. Limitations on these various defects are governed by AWS D1.1, the ASME Boiler and Pressure Vessel Code, or MIL-R-11468, where the acceptance level depends on the application.

b. Cracking. Cracking is one of the flaws that occurs most often in weldments. Cracks occur when the temperature of the cooling weld and base plate is within either of two ranges. One is at or slightly below the solidification temperature of the weld metal, and the other is from about 4000 F to ambient temperature. The high temperature cracking is called hot tearing and occurs because the metal is weak and has limited plasticity at this temperature. Fillet welds, weld craters, and the heat-affected zone display this type of cracking. Low-temperature cracking, or cold cracking, occurs in root passes of butt welds and in the heat-affected zone, and is invariably associated with the presence of hydrogen as a dissolved impurity.

(1) Hot tearing. High-temperature cracks are intercrystalline tears that occur at or near the range of solidification for the metal. They are attributed to the presence of low-freezing compounds such as iron sulfide, or solid impurities that have little or no tensile strength or plasticity at high temperatures. These tears are in the metal that is last to freeze in the weld deposit. Sulfur contributes significantly to hot tearing, while silicon, phosphorus, carbon, copper, and nickel have a lesser role. Manganese, on the other hand, has a beneficial effect on hot ductility because it has a greater affinity to sulfur than iron does. Manganese sulfides form; these have a higher melting temperature than steel and produce globular inclusions rather than the intergranular film that iron sulfide forms. If the ratio of manganese to sulfur in steel is 60 or greater, then hot tearing is not likely to occur. Electrodes recommended by AWS D1.1 or the ASME Boiler and Pressure Vessel Code, as

appropriate, will produce a weld deposit with minimum hot cracking tendencies. Preheating, controlling interpass temperature, and welding with as little restraint as possible are other ways to control hot cracking, particularly in a section thickness greater than 1/2 inch.

(2) Cold cracking.

(a) Cold cracking occurs in the heat-affected zone and weld metal. This may be caused by mechanical effects, alloy content, or hydrogen pickup from moisture in the electrode flux or on surfaces of the weld joint. Mechanically, high shrinkage stresses are induced in the weld metal by the cooling weld and the restraining action of the base metal. These stresses act in directions parallel and perpendicular to the weld and their magnitude may be great enough to cause cracking.

(b) In any thickness of steel, cold cracking may also occur 'in the heat-affected zone because of alloy content. This is called underbead cracking. The higher the alloy content, the greater the tendency. Susceptibility to underbead cracking maybe estimated from a steel's "carbon equivalent, " which is determined from the formula:

$$\text{Carbon equivalent (C.E.)} = \%C + \frac{\%Mn}{6} + \frac{\%Cr + \%Mo + \%V}{10}$$

As the C.E. increases, so does the susceptibility of the steel to cold cracking. As a steel's alloy content, or C. E., increases, its capability to form a hardened microstructure such as martensite when cooled rapidly also increases. Certain areas of the weld joint, particularly those next to the base metal heat-affected zone, may cool rapidly enough to produce a hardened structure which becomes a "metallurgical notch. " This hardened zone may be brittle, with a characteristic low notch toughness. Increasing the heat input or the preheat/interpass temperature will slow the cooling rate. However, high-strength, low-alloy steels should be preheated carefully so the steel in the heat-affected zone will not be weakened. This precaution also applies to the use of interpass temperature, air-arc gouging, post weld heating, and heat input during welding. Removal of defects, when repair is permitted, should be by grinding or air-arc gouging followed by grinding to limit the heat input effects of the gouging. Steel manufacturers should be consulted for recommendations about weld repairs. Few of the steels used in bridge or building construction and piping systems have enough alloying elements to create a problem with hardening in the heat-affected zone. Occasionally,

however, a designer might specify a steel that can harden quickly enough to require preheating. Preheat temperatures for many of the steels are listed in the following documents: structural steels — AWS D1.1; piping materials — ANSI B31.1; ferrous materials — ASME Boiler and Pressure Vessel Code, section HI, appendix III, "Other Applications, " and the text *Weldability* of *Steels,* edited by Stout and Doty (1971).

(c) Hydrogen also contributes to cold cracking. Three factors act simultaneously in hydrogen-induced cracking: dissolved hydrogen, tensile stresses, and a low-ductility microstructure such as martensite. The source of hydrogen is the shield gas, flux, or surface contamination. The hydrogen is carried as a diatomic molecule to the arc and is converted to the monatomic or ionized state. The monatomic hydrogen readily dissolves in the molten weld metal. The exact mechanism by which hydrogen causes cold cracking has not been fully explained. But many investigators believe that as the weld metal cools, it becomes supersaturated, and the hydrogen diffuses to a highly stressed area such as the heat-affected zone or the atmosphere. Once in the heat-affected zone, it is theorized that the hydrogen embrittles the metal. Some low-alloy steels, such as ASTM A 514 or A 517, will transform to martensite under rapid cooling conditions, and at the same time will entrap some or all of the hydrogen present. However, hydrogen has low volubility in the martensitic structure and tends to migrate to any neighboring discontinuities. Along with external forces, the hydrogen enlarges these flaws to a critical size. Regardless of the mechanism by which hydrogen embrittles the carbon and low-alloy steels, however, precautions should be taken against its entrainment. Joint design and attention to joint fit-up can reduce the chances of cold cracking. To control hydrogen-induced cracking, a post-weld temperature of 300 to 400 "F for up to 10 hours (depending on weld thickness) is recommended. This technique should be specified with caution because of the risks noted in (3) below. Cleaning joints to remove hydrogen-containing materials such as oil and grease, and using of low hydrogen electrodes are also recommended to limit the source of hydrogen.

(3) Reheat cracking. Reheat cracking occurs in steels containing carbide-forming alloy elements such as vanadium or molybdenum. When a post-weld heat treatment is used, these materials often exhibit precipitation of alloy carbides that make the grains of the heat-affected zone stronger than the grain boundaries. If there are stresses, the grain

boundary region must adjust to relieve them. Extensive deformation in the grain boundary region may induce cracking, especially in the heat-affected zone. The risk of reheat cracking can be reduced by using electrodes that do not have yield strengths much higher than that of the base plate, by avoiding highly rigid joint details in thick plate, by grinding butt welds flush, and by smoothing the contour of fillet welds, especially the toe of the weld. The AWS D1.1 section "Workmanship — Stress Relief Heat Treatment," and ASME Boiler and Pressure Vessel Code, section VIII, "Procedures on Post-Weld Heat Treatment" contain recommended practices for heat-treating welds for stress relief. The stress-relief heat treatment of quenched and tempered ASTM A 514 and A 517 steels is not usually recommended but may be required to maintain dimensional stability during machining.

c. Other defects. Other defects can be introduced into the weld metal if the proper weld process or technique is not used. These defects include porosity, slag inclusions, incomplete fusion, inadequate joint penetration, and undercut. Each of these is described in paragraph 4-2e.

5-3. Joint design

Weld joints are prepared either by flame cutting or mechanically by machining or grinding, depending on the joint details. Before welding, the joint surfaces must be cleared of all foreign materials such as paint, dirt, scale, or rust. Suitable solvents or light grinding can be used for cleaning. The joint surface should not be nicked or gouged since they can interfere with the welding operation.

5-4. Methods of welding carbon steels and low-alloy steels

Carbon and low-alloy steels are readily welded in the field by SMAW, GMAW, FCAW or SAW. SMAW is used most often because the equipment is simple and portable. GMAW, FCAW, and SAW are being used more often in the field because of weld quality and economics. Standard joint designs for these processes are in the AWS D1.1 section "Design of Welded Connections," and ASME Boiler and Pressure Vessel Code, subsection B, "Joint Details for Pressure Vessels. " Recommended preheat temperatures for commonly used steels are also given in the codes; these figures are based on plate thickness and the ambient temperature. Recommended preheat temperatures for various steels are listed in the AWS D1.1 section, "Technique," and appendix R of the ASME Boiler and Pressure Vessel Code.

5-5. Shielded metal-arc (SMAW)

SMAW has been the preferred method of welding because of its versatility, the simplicity of its equipment, and the wide selection of electrodes, All of these characteristics are important for field weld applications. AWS A5.1 and A5.5 specify mild steel and low-alloy steel SMAW electrodes.

a. Electrode classification system. The AWS has developed a classification system which describes some of the characteristics of steel welding electrodes. The SMAW classification codes are made up of an E and four and five numbers (EXXYZ). The E indicates that the material is an electrode. The first two digits, xX, give the minimum tensile strength of the weld deposit in 1000 pounds per square inch (psi); that is, an electrode with an E70YZ classification would have a minimum tensile strength of 70,000 psi. The tensile strength designation starts at 60 and increases by 10 to 120. The number represented by Y can be either 1 or 2 and designates the proper welding positions for this electrode type. A 1 means that the electrode can be used in all positions: flat, horizontal, vertical, and overhead; a 2 indicates that it can be used only on flat or horizontal fillet welds, The last term in the classification, Z, can be any number from O through 8. These numbers, identified in AWS A5.1, indicate major coating constituents and welding current types.

b. Chemical requirements. The AWS divides SMAW electrodes into two groups: mild steel (AWS A5.1) and low-alloy steel (AWS A5.5). The E60XX and E70XX electrodes are in the mild steel specification. The chemical requirements for E70XX electrodes are listed in AWS A5.1 and allow for wide variations of composition of the deposited weld metal. There are no specified chemical requirements for the E60XX electrodes. The low-alloy specification contains electrode classifications E70XX through El 20XX. These codes have a suffix indicating the chemical requirements of the class of electrodes — for example, E7010-A1 or E8018-C1. The composition of low-alloy E70XX electrodes is controlled much more closely than that of mild steel E70XX electrodes. Low-alloy electrodes of the low-hydrogen classification (EXX15, EXX16, EXX18) require special handling to help the coatings from picking up water. Manufacturers' recommendations about storage and rebaking must be followed for these electrodes. AWS A5.5 provides a specific listing of chemical requirements.

c. Weld metal mechanical property requirements. The AWS requires the deposited weld metal to have minimum tensile and impact strengths. The detailed requirements for mild steel electrodes are listed in

AWS A5.1, and for low-alloy steel electrodes in AWS A5.5.

d. Recommended filler metals for commonly used steels. Commonly used ASTM and API steels, and matching filler metal requirements are listed in the table "Matching Filler Metal Requirements" of AWS D1.1. This document lists the steel and minimum preheat and interpass temperatures for different plate thicknesses and welding processes. If a steel is not listed, manufacturers' recommendations should be followed. AWS A5.1 contains the intended use of the electrodes as an appendix. Chemical composition also should be considered when low-alloy electrodes are specified.

5-6. Gas metal-arc (GMAW)

GMAW is being used more often for shop and field applications because it is more economical than SMAW. With GMAW, there is much less downtime for electrode changes, much less loss due to stub ends and spatter, and much less interpass cleaning required. GMAW is also slightly less versatile because the welding gun is bulkier than the electrode holder for SMAW. However, GMAW can be used in all positions with either short-circuiting transfer or a pulsed voltage power supply. The equipment is more complex and more expensive than that for SMAW, and requires more skill on the part of the operator.

a. Electrode classification system. The classification codes for GMAW electrode wire consist of an E and four digits in the configuration EXXY-Z. As with SMAW, the E indicates an electrode, and XX gives the deposited tensile strength in 10,000-psi increments. The tensile strength designations range from 70 to 110. The next digit, Y, can be either an S or a U. The S indicates a solid bare wire, while U means that the solid wire has an emissive coating that allows the use of DC straight polarity. The final digit, Z, can be any number from 1 through 6 or the letter G. The numbers indicate chemical analysis, particularly carbon and silicon. The G classification has no chemical requirements. The letter B at the end of the code, such as E70S-1B, indicates a low-alloy steel electrode. Only the E70S-X and E70U-1 electrodes are specified by AWS AS.18.

b. Chemical requirements. The chemical requirements for the GMAW electrodes are presented in AWS AS. 18. The E70S-G and E70S-GB electrodes have no chemical requirements, except that no additions of nickel, chromium, molybdenum, or vanadium are allowed. Chemical requirements for the higher-strength low-alloy electrodes are in MIL-E-18193, MIL-E-19822, MIL-E-23765/1, and MIL-E-

23765/2. All chemical analyses are based on the as-manufactured electrode wire.

c. Weld metal mechanical properties. The all-weld metal tensile properties for the E70 electrodes are presented in AWS A5.18.

d. Shielding gas. Two shield gasses are used with GMAW—carbon dioxide, and argon plus 1 to 5 percent oxygen addition. Carbon dioxide is used for short-circuiting transfer and for flat-position welding. Argon-oxygen shield gas is used with pulsed voltage out-of-position welding and spray transfer welding. The GMAW electrodes and recommended shield gases are listed in AWS A5.18.

e. Recommended filler metals for commonly used steels. The table "Matching Filler Metal Requirements" in AWS D1.1 lists commonly used steels by ASTM and API specification numbers, and gives matching filler metal requirements and classifications. In addition, AWS D1.1 lists the steels and the minimum preheat and interpass temperatures for different plate thicknesses and welding processes. If steels other than those listed are used, manufacturers' recommendations for weld metals and preheat temperature should be followed. The intended uses of the electrode types are indicated in an appendix to AWS A5.18.

5-7. Flux-cored arc welding (FCAW)

FCAW which uses equipment similar to that of GMAW, is advantageous because it provides high deposition and fluxing ingredients. This process is primarily for flat and horizontal welds, but can be used in other positions if the proper electrode diameter and welding currents are selected. Mild steel FCAW electrodes are specified by AWS A5.20. Low-alloy FCAW electrodes are available; manufacturers' recommendations for their use should be followed.

a. Electrode classification system. The FCAW electrodes are classified similarly to the GMAW electrodes. In the code EXXT-Y, the EXX designation is the same as for SMAW and GMAW electrodes and can be either E60T-Y or E70T-Y. The letter T indicates a continuous tubular electrode with a powdered flux filling the tube. The suffix Y, which can be any number from 1 through 8 or the letter G, indicates the deposited weld metal chemistry and shielding gas used.

b. Chemical requirements. The deposited weld metal chemical analysis for mild steel FCAW electrodes is in AWS A5.20. There are no chemical requirements for E70T-2, E70T-3, and E70T-G electrodes.

c. Weld metal mechanical properties. The all-weld metal tensile and impact requirements for the mild steel FCAW electrodes are presented in AWS A5.20.

d. Shielding gas. The FCAW electrodes use carbon dioxide for shielding gas or contain in the flux gas-producing compounds that protect the arc from atmospheric contamination. The E60T-7, E60T-8, E70T-4, and E70T-6 electrodes need no external shield gas. The E70T-1 and E70T-2 electrodes need additional shielding from carbon dioxide. The E70T-5 electrode can be used with or without carbon dioxide as a separate shield gas. The shielding gas for the E70T-G electrode is not specified.

e. Recommended filler metals for commonly used steels. Commonly used steels are listed by ASTM and API specification numbers in the table "Matching Filler Metal Requirements" of AWS D1.1. This specification also gives the matching filler metal requirements and the electrode classifications that meet those requirements. Electrodes E70T-2 and E70T-3 are not recommended by the AWS Code. The table "Minimum Preheat and Interpass Temperature" in AWS D1.1 categorizes commonly used steels, plate thicknesses, and welding processes with their associated preheat and interpass temperatures. If steels other than those listed are to be used, manufacturer's recommendations for weld metal and preheat temperatures should be followed. AWS A5.20 for FCAW electrodes contains an appendix that lists the intended use of the electrodes.

5-8. Submerged arc (SAW)

SAW is limited to flat and horizontal fillet welding because a granulated flux is used to protect the arc and the molten weld metal. SAW electrodes and flux for mild steel are specifed by AWS A5.17. Low-alloy weld metal is specified in AWS A5.23.

a. Material classification. The classification system for submerged arc electrodes and fluxes has two parts; the first refers to the flux and the second to the electrode. Thus, the classification has the following: FXX-EXXX. The F indicates that the material is a flux. The first number indicates the minimum deposited weld metal tensile strength in 10,000-psi increments. This digit can be any number from 6 to 12. The last number of this part indicates the impact requirements of the deposited weld metal. Examples of flux designations are F61, F86, or F128. The next part of the classification begins with an E and designates an electrode. For mild steel, a three- to five-digit code is used. The first digit, either an L,

M, or H, indicates the relative manganese content of the electrode wire. The next one or two digits give the nominal carbon content of the electrode wire. The code may be followed by a K, which shows the wire was made from a silicon-killed heat of steel. Examples of mild steel codes would be EL8K or EM12. Low-alloy electrodes have similar coding systems, with the E again indicating an electrode. The next two or three digits indicate the as-manufactured wire chemistry. The final part indicates the deposited weld metal chemistry. This part of the coding system applies to low-alloy classification only; the suffix N indicates the material is nuclear grade. Examples of SAW classifications are F70-EL12-A1, combination for carbon-molybdenum low-alloy steels; F86-EB2-B2, combination for chromium-molybdenum low-alloy steels; or F61-EM12K, combination for mild steel.

b. Chemical requirements. The electrode chemical composition requirements are presented in AWS A5.17 for mild steel and AWS A5.23 for low-alloy steels. The deposited weld metal chemical requirements are presented in AWS A5.23 for alloy steels. The only chemical composition requirement for fluxes is that the combination of a flux and low-alloy steel electrode produce a specified deposited weld metal chemistry.

c. Weld metal mechanical properties. The all-weld metal tensile and impact requirements for mild and low-alloy steel welds are presented in AWS A5.17 and A5.23, respectively. The EXXX after the flux designation means that the flux will produce these strengths when used in combination with any electrode.

d. Recommended filler metal for commonly used steels. The table "Matching Filler Metal Requirements" in AWS D1.1 lists the ASTM and API classifications of commonly used steels, the matching filler metal requirements, and the electrode classifications that meet these requirements. The table "Minimum Preheat and Interpass" in AWS D1.1 lists the steels, the minimum preheat and interpass temperatures for a range of plate thicknesses, and the various welding processes. If steels other than those listed are to be used, then manufacturer's recommendations for weld metals and preheat temperatures should be followed. The appendices of AWS A5.17 and A5.23 list usages and choice of fluxes for the SAW process.

CHAPTER 6

WELDING ALUMINUM ALLOYS

6-1. General

The aluminum alloys commonly used in constructing pressure vessels, cryogenic vessels, piping systems, and accessories are specified by the Aluminum Association, Inc. (AA), ASTM, and military or other Federal specifications . Aluminum welding electrodes and filler rods are specified in AWS A5.10 or military documents.

6-2. Weldability of aluminum alloys

a. Introduction. Most aluminum alloys can be joined by either GMAW or the GTAW processes. The weldability of aluminum alloys is essentially the same for both processes. The most easily welded alloys are those of the non-heat-treatable lXXX, 3XXX, and 5 XXX series, and the heat-treatable 6XXX series; of the 7XXX series, only two alloys (7005 and 7039) were developed specifically for welding.

(1) Non-heat-treatable alloys. The composition of non-heat-treatable aluminum alloys determines their relative mechanical strength, which increases with cold work (H temper) or strain hardening. Alloys in the annealed (O temper) condition have the weakest mechanical properties. Magnesium-containing alloys (5XXX) are typically given a low-temperature stabilization treatment. This lowers the strength slightly but increases ductility and produces some precipitation. Reheating or annealing weakens strain-hardened material.

(2) Heat-treatable alloys. Appropriate solution, quenching, and precipitation reactions produce heat-treatable alloys with maximum strength. This age-hardening mechanism requires an alloying element with appreciable solid volubility in aluminum at elevated temperatures, but with limited solubilities at lower temperatures. Typically, thermal treatments first involve solution heat treatment; that is, heating to the 900 to 1000 °F range but below the eutectic melting temperature. At these temperatures, the maximum amount of solute is taken into solution (W temper). By quenching from the solution treating temperature, a nonequilibrium, supersaturated solid solution is obtained. Quenching rate is critical for some alloy compositions, particularly through the 550 to 750 'F range. The degree of quench sensitivity depends on alloy composition. Some precipitation from the supersaturated solid solution at room temperature strengthens the alloy. However, this natural aging will approach a maximum strength in time (T4 temper). Of course, the rate of natural aging and the strengths produced vary with alloy composition. Holding at reduced temperatures will slow precipitation of the material undergoing natural aging. If the material which has been solution heat treated and quenched is heated typicall y to the 300 to 500 °F range, desirable precipitation occurs. This markedly increases the alloy's mechanical properties (T6 temper). Heating a t higher temperatures (500 to 800 "F) results in non-strengthening precipitation of the solute element. This annealing treatment tends to produce an equilibrium structure with high ductility and low strength (O temper).

b. Welding procedures. Welding procedures should be qualified before work proceeds on the structure (chapter 2). The welding procedures depend on the base plate, the structure being welded, the position of the weld (i.e., flat, overhead, horizontal, or vertical), and the chemical composition of the metal. For proper welding, aluminum must be clean. All foreign matter must be removed from the joint area so that the contaminants do not become fluid from the heat of welding and flow into the joint. Cleaning is most effective just before welding; however, the welding supervisor can set a suitable time limit based on shop conditions and requirements of the product. Three methods are commonly used to clean aluminum: solvent decreasing, mechanical cleaning, and chemical etch cleaning.

(1) Solvent decreasing to remove grease, oil, dirt, and loose particles is most effective when the metal surface is smooth and when contaminants are not tightly adhered. Solvents include a wide range of commercial products — e.g., acetone and clorothene NU. But one should not use hydrocarbons such as carbon tetrachloride and trichloroethylene; these break down in the presence of the welding arc to form highly toxic gases such as phosgene. Safety precautions should be observed when using all solvents.

(2) Mechanical methods of cleaning include wire brushing, scraping, filing, planing, grinding, and rubbing with steel wool. Because these methods are costly, they should be used only for the weld

areas. wire brushing may be done with a hard brush or power rotary brush. Both types should have stainless steel bristles. These brushes must be kept clean; when the bristles become dirty, they must be degreased with solvents like those discussed above. Before brushing, the joint area should be degreased. If this is done, the brush will stay clean and will not drive contaminants into the aluminum surface. Burnishing the aluminum surface can also entrap contaminants; therefore, only light pressure should be used for power brushing. Cleaning by grinding is best done with an open-coat aluminum oxide disk (80 grit). This process is especially useful for removing the heavy oxide film associated with water staining; wire brushing and chemical etching are not effective. After mechanical cleaning, the metal should be degreased.

(3) Chemical etching, which is useful for batch cleaning, produces a surface free from contaminants and heavy oxide films. However, etched surfaces tend to be more absorptive than before. Thus, they can be recontaminated if not protected and should be cleaned just before welding.

(4) Following improper procedures — particularly when cleaning — can produce defects in the weld joint. These include porosity, tungsten inclusions, incomplete fusion, inadequate joint penetration, undercutting, and cracking. Limitations on various defects are governed by the ASME Boiler and Pressure Vessel Code or military specifications; whether a defect is severe enough to be unacceptable depends on the function of the finished product.

c. Cracking. Sensitivity to weld cracking largely depends on the weld metal's composition. Both base metal and filler alloy composition affect the resulting weld bead composition, and the welding heat input affects the relative percentages of base metal and filler metal in the weld bead. Furthermore, joint design can significantly influence the relative percentage of base metal melted. In most alloy systems, there are one or more regions of maximum crack sensitivity. If the base metal composition has a high cracking sensitivity, then filler alloys containing high percentages of magnesium are used. This changes the composition so that the weld metal is less sensitive to cracking. Minor alloying elements also change weld crack sensitivity. In particular, grain-refining elements such as Titanium and Zirconium are frequently added to reduce the cracking tendencies of filler alloys. Minor amounts of copper in an aluminum-magnesium-zinc alloy greatly increase crack sensitivity. The copper contributes to the formation of low-melting phases that segregate at grain boundaries. Shrinkage stresses during weld solidification can then cause boundary separation before this low-melting phase solidifies.

(1) Crater cracks. Crater cracks are most often encountered in aluminum welding. These are small checks or crow's foot defects which occur during solidification after the welding arc has been broken Such cracks may be small but are very serious since they are usually at the end of a weld, where stress concentration or "end effect" is most pronounced. The number of crater cracks can be limited with good welding practice. This usually involves proper manipulation of the torch or filler, or both. The technique most often used is to break and restart the arc several times so that the shrinkage pipe in the center is filled. In addition, run-out tabs are often used to prevent crater cracks. The welder should check carefully for these cracks, and should remove them before rewelding. It is very hard to remove a crater crack by remelting the weld.

(2) Longitudinal cracking. Cold longitudinal cracks are not usually found in aluminum welds, but hot cracks can sometimes occur when the metal is passing between the liquidus and solidus temperatures. These cracks usually are caused by incorrect filler alloy, too low or too high a welding rate, and incorrect edge preparation or joint spacing. Cold cracks which occur below the solidus temperature usually result w-hen too small a weld bead is laid down. Cold cracks can be eliminated by a weld bead large enough to withstand the cooling stresses encountered during solidification.

d. Other defects. Other defects can be introduced into the weld metal if an improper weld process or technique is used. These defects include porosity, tungsten inclusions, incomplete fusion, inadequate joint penetration, and undercut. Paragraph 4-2e discusses incomplete fusion, inadequate joint penetration, and undercutting. This information applies to aluminum as well as stainless steel.

(1) Porosity. Shrinkage porosity, associated with overheating, and gas porosity are common defects in welds. Spherical gas pores are found most often hydrogen is accepted as the major cause of porosity in aluminum welds. Hydrogen usually results from water or hydrocarbon contamination of the base plate, filler wire, shielding gas, or arc column. The size and number of gas pores for an existing hydrogen concentration vary with the weld metal's solidification rate. Porosity formation is a nucleation and growth process. At fast solidification rates, there is not enough time for the nucleation step, and no pores can be seen -- even at high hydrogen concentrations. At slower solidification rates, pore nucleation and some growth occur, but the bubbles are trapped in the freezing metal before escaping. At

slower and slower solidification rates, more time is available for pores to grow and for gas to escape from the molten pool. When solidification rates are slow enough, all gas escapes and no porosity remains in the weld bead. Random, scattered porosity that is usually detected radiographically has little effect on the mechanical properties. Of course, larger amounts of gross porosity reduce the metal's cross-sectional area and lower the weld's strength. Aligned or layered porosity has a greater effect on mechanical properties. Microporosity, too small to be detected by standard radiographic techniques, typically occurs in layers along the weld fusion line. This defect lowers mechanical properties considerably.

(2) Tungsten inclusions. Tungsten inclusions occur only when the GTAW process is used. The tungsten becomes trapped in the molten weld metal because of two transfer processes. If the electrode's diameter is too small, the welding current melts too much of the end, and any mechanical jostling of the torch will cause a droplet of tungsten to be transferred to the weld puddle. Tungsten also can be transferred if the electrode is touched to the weld metal. To prevent tungsten inclusions, electrodes with the correct diameter and with the proper taper ground on the end should be used.

6-3. Joint design

Weld joints are prepared mechanically by machining, grinding, or plasma cutting. Before welding, the joint surfaces must be cleared of all foreign materials such as paint, dirt, scale, or oxide; solvent cleaning, light grinding, or etching can be used. The joint surfaces should not be nicked or gouged since this can hinder welding. The AWS *Welding Handbook,* Chapter 69, "Aluminum and Aluminum Alloys" has a section on designing joints for welding. The theory and practice of designing aluminum structures are discussed; joint accessibility, edge preparation, and stress distribution are covered.

6-4. Methods of welding aluminum alloys

The best welds result from careful cleaning of the joint, proper selection of filler wire, and good welding practice. Aluminum alloys can be welded by several processes. The choice depends on conditions such as thickness and size of parts, location and position of weld, number of similar welds, production rate required, finish and appearance desired, and type of aluminum alloy. The welding processes which have been successful are gas, carbon arc, atomic hydrogen, GTAW, and GMAW. The inert

shielded-arc welding process can be used in all positions, including overhead. Aluminum alloys for cryogenic applications are welded by either the GTAW or the GMAW processes. This manual discusses only the inert shielded-arc welding processes, the most versatile and commonly used for field fabrication. Preheating the weld joint before welding is not recommended. But if ambient temperatures are low, a preheat of not more than 300 "F can be applied to the joint before welding. The properties and metallurgy of aluminum alloys are almost always affected adversely by elevated temperatures, Therefore preheating is not recommended, and welding heat should be applied as briefly as possible.

6-5. Gas metal-arc (GMAW)

Use of GMAW is increasing for shop and field applications because of the economics of the process. There is less downtime for electrode changes, much less loss due to stub ends and spatter, and much less interpass cleaning required. GMAW can be used in all positions, with either short circuiting transfer or a pulsed voltage power supply. No flux is required for welding aluminum with the GMAW process. This eliminates costly flux removal and the possibility of post-weld corrosion due to flux residue. Another outstanding characteristic of the GMAW process is its use of high welding current densities. Current densities on the wire commonly range from 60,000 to 300,000 amperes per square inch. These high current densities, coupled with a very efficient heat transfer in the arc, result in higher welding speeds, less distortion, lower welding costs, better mechanical strength, and better corrosion resistance than can be obtained with any other arc welding process on aluminum. High current densities and the efficient heat transfer in the arc also produce deep penetration. This makes the process good for fillet welds and reduces the need for edge preparation. For more details, refer to chapter 3.

a. Electrode classification system. The classification codes for GMAW electrode wire consist of an E, an R, and four digits in the configuration ERXXXX. The prefix R indicates that the material is suitable for use as a welding rod, and the prefix E indicates suitability as an electrode. These filler metals can be used as electrodes in GMAW and as welding rods in GTAW; both letters (ER) indicate suitability either as a welding rod or an electrode. So, an electrode which meets the test prescribed in AWS A5.10 always can be used as either an electrode or a welding rod. The four numbers in the electrode classification system refer to the alloy chemistry of the rod or electrode. For example, an ER1100 classification would be an electrode or rod having a chemical make-up equivalent to the 1100 alloy of aluminum.

b. Chemical requirements. AWS A5.10 contains the chemical requirements for GMAW electrodes. The proportions of elements are similar in electrodes and base metals with the same designation. All chemical analyses are based on the as-manufactured electrode wire.

c. Weld metal mechanical properties. For aluminum weld metal, AWS A5.10 specifies only ductility as measured by the bend test, but not strength or impact resistance levels.

d. Shielding gas. Helium and argon are the shield gases for the CMAW process. Argon is used more often now, but the availability and use of helium are increasing rapidly. Because of helium's low density, a greater volume is required to produce the necessary shielding. But deeper weld penetration is possible because of helium's higher ionization potential. Argon is better for manual welding because of the arc instability y with pure helium. Helium/argon mixtures are being used more for semiautomatic welding, while both mixtures and pure helium are widely used for automatic welding. To obtain adequate weld penetration, helium alone — or a mixture of helium and argon — may be preferred for welding very heavy sections (more than 2 inches), This mixture, 75 percent helium and 25 percent argon, is commonly used and is available premixed.

e. Recommended filler metals for aluminum alloy welding. The aluminum alloys are listed by the AA specification numbers in the table entitled "Guide to the Choice of Filler Metal for General Purpose Welding," appendix 1 of AWS A5.10. They are also in the AWS *Welding Handbook,* Chapter 69, "Aluminum and Aluminum Alloys" and ASM *Metals Handbook, Volume 6, Arc Welding of Aluminum Alloys.*

6-6. Gas tungsten-arc (GTAW)

GTAW of aluminum is done with AC and superimposed high frequency in an atmosphere of argon gas. In some industries, GTAW with DC straight polarity and helium gas is receiving increased attention. DC GTAW is done only with very low currents because of overheating in the electrode. However, this process is seldom used because of the accumulation of tungsten inclusions noted in paragraph 6-2. As with the GMAW process, GTAW does not use fluxes; the welding arc in argon gas removes the aluminum oxide film from the surface of the metal, and the argon shield prevents it from reforming. GTAW welds have good appearance and require little, if any, grinding or finishing. The GTAW process can produce X-ray quality welds in all the weldable aluminum alloys. Under proper conditions, GTAW welds may have a sounder structure than welds made with most other processes. Excellent penetration is easily obtained on butt welds that have been properly prepared. However, care and experience are required to obtain adequate penetration on fillet and lap welds since there is a tendency to bridge the root unless adequate current and a short arc are maintained, AC GTAW is usually confined to thicknesses below 1/4 inch. The GMAW process or DC straight polarity GTAW is generally for thicker sections. GTAW welding is normally used for most pipe welding, for joints where abrupt changes in direction of the weld are encountered, and almost always for welding aluminum less than 1/16-inch thick. High quality welds can be made in all positions. For additional information on welding process, see chapter 3.

a. Electrode classification system. The classification code for the GTAW filler rod consists of an E, an R, and four digits in the configuration ERXXXX. The letter E indicates that this is an electrode material, and the R indicates that it is a welding rod. Since these filler metals can be used as GMAW electrodes as well as filler rods for GTAW, both letters are used. The four-digit number, such as 1100 in ER1100, designates the chemical composition of the filler metal. The specification for these electrodes is in AWS A5.10.

b. Chemical requirements. The chemical compositions for GTAW welding rods are listed in AWS A5.10. The proportions of elements are similar in electrodes and base metals with the same four-digit designation. All chemical analyses are based on the as-manufactured welding rod.

c. Weld metal mechanical properties. For aluminum weld metal, AWS A5.10 specifies only ductility as measured by the bend test, but not strength or impact resistance levels.

d. Shielding gas. Two shield gases are used with the GTAW process: pure argon and pure helium. Argon is for thicknesses of 1/4 inch and less. Pure helium is for thicker material when DC straight polarity is used, and for machine welds.

e. Recommended filler metals for aluminum alloys. The aluminum alloys are listed by AA specification numbers in the table entitled "Guide to the Choice of Filler Metal for General Purpose Welding" in AWS A5.10, Appendix 1. A comprehensive list is also in the AWS *Welding Handbook,* Chapter 69, "Aluminum and Aluminum Alloys" and ASM *Handbook,* Volume 6, "Arc Welding of Aluminum Alloys."

CHAPTER 7

WELDING FOR SPECIAL APPLICATIONS

7-1. General

This chapter discusses welding applications for concrete reinforcing steel bars, railroad and crane rails, castings, and composite materials. For these applications welding procedures must be qualified by suitable tests (appendix B), and persons skilled in the specific process being used must do the welding.

7-2. Reinforcing steel bars

The widespread use of large-diameter and high-strength reinforcing bars has made welded splices very important. Welding is required where it is hard or impractical to overlap bars and rely on the surrounding concrete to transmit the load from one bar to the other. Yet many of the reinforcing steels are classified as hard to weld because of unfavorable chemical composition (a high carbon equivalent). Some specifications prohibit arc welding of reinforcing steels whose carbon contents exceed 0.50 percent.

a. Procedures. Welded splices in reinforcing steel bars have been used successfully since the middle 1930s. SMAW and thermit welding have been the most popular methods of joining reinforcing bars for field construction; the pressure gas and SAW processes are for shop welding. GMAW and FCAW also have been used successfully in the past few years,

(1) When reinforcing bars for concrete are to be welded, one must determine the steel's composition and matching welding procedures, However, it is hard to positively identify new and used reinforcing bars, especially those to which splices are being made so that a structure can be enlarged or modified. Even after positive identification of the reinforcing bar, the question of steel chemistry may remain; reinforcing bars usually conform to ASTM standards, which base the requirements on physical properties and often do not specify steel chemistry.

(2) Welding should conform to AWS D12.1. This specification deals with permissible stresses, including unit stresses in welds; effective weld areas, lengths, and throat thicknesses; structural details for welding transitions in bar sizes, splice qualifications, indirect butt splice details, and lap welded splice details; and interconnections of precast members. AWS D12.1 also discusses workmanship, technique, qualification, and inspection of the joints.

b. Strength requirement, The strength of welded splices in reinforcing steel bars can be determined by the ultimate strength method or the working stress method. AWS D12.1, table 2-2, describes the type of joint and weld, the base metal used, and the two methods of determining strength for both direct and indirect butt splices. The requirement for transition strength levels is also discussed in American Concrete Institute (ACI) 318.

c. Welding processes. Joints in reinforcing steel bars can be made in several ways: SMAW, GMAW, FCAW, thermit welding, or pressure gas welding. AWS D12.1, section 5, details the procedures to be used with the various welding processes. AWS D12.1, table 5.1, shows the various types of electrode materials to be used with the three arc welding processes. Thermit and pressure gas welding do not require these filler metals. AWS D12.1, table 5.2, shows the preheat temperatures to be used for various carbon equivalents for reinforcing bars of different sizes.

d. Mechanical butt splices. Butt splices in reinforcing steel bars can also be made mechanically. A splicing method has been developed which uses the exothermic process; molten filler metal is put in the annular space between the bar and high-strength steel sleeve with an inside diameter larger than the overall diameter of the bar. Since the strength of the joint does not depend on fusion of the filler metal to the reinforcing steel or the sleeve, this is classified as a mechanical joint rather than a welded splice,

e. Contract specifications. Contract specifications should include requirements for procedure qualification, welder or welding operator qualification, and inspection. The inspection should cover the materials, the equipment necessary to conduct the welding procedure, the qualifications of the welder or welding operator, and the completed work and records, The qualification tests must be conducted on the same material that will be used in the actual construction. Requirements for the welding procedure should cover the material specification, the welding process to be used, the position of the weld, the filler metal classification, and the type of pass (single- or multi-pass). The procedure should also include requirements for a preheat-interpass temperature and a post-weld heat treatment, if required.

7-3. Rail

a. *Advantages of welding.* Welding railroad and crane rail joints offers several advantages. Continuous rails need less maintenance and wear less than rails that have joint ends with bolted connections. Loads roll smoothly from joint to joint. Most railroad rail is welded in-shop in l/4-mile lengths by either pressure gas welding or flash welding. Welding in the field can be done using the exothermic process described in the AWS *Welding Handbook,* section 2.

b. *Exothermic welding.* Exothermic welding is the only rail welding process covered in this manual, since the other processes are primarily limited to shop welding. For exothermic welding, the ends of the rails must be clean; the joint faces parallel, properly gapped, and aligned; and the joint preheated. However, production joints made in the shop or in the field do not necessarily produce consistent strength, so the following precautions should be taken.

(1) Detailed welding procedures must be prepared. All procedures for production welding must be qualified before welding starts. Completed welds should be visually inspected. If there are blowouts or voids, the welded joint should be replaced.

(2) Visual inspection must not be used for acceptance of the completed weld. Internal defects such as lack of fusion, slag inclusion, porosity, and cracks might not be visible. Unfortunately, no methods are entirely suitable for inspecting rail welds made by the exothermic process.

(3) Radiographic and ultrasonic inspection must be included in contract specifications. However, these approaches are not completely satisfactory. In radiographic examination, excess metal must be removed from the web of the rail and the joint ground smooth. However, since varying thicknesses are still involved, this method is hard to use and results may be inconclusive. portable ultrasonic inspection equipment is commercially available; but it is very sensitive if improperly set up and may indicate nonexistent or insignificant defects. Magnetic particle inspection is used for gas-pressure-welded and flash-welded rail but is not as suitable for rail welds made by the exothermic process. Railroad personnel generally use Sperry Rail Detector cars to inspect rails when the track is being used.

(4) Room for thermal expansion must be provided when continuously welded rail is designed and constructed. This is normally done by restraining the rail by joint-bar friction at the ends and then subjecting it to accumulated restraint from successive ties. Rails are usually laid so as to give zero restraint at the anticipated mean temperature. Short buffer rails, which are frequently installed at regular intervals along the track, allow 3/8-inch movement of each rail end without bending the joint bolts. These buffer rails make adjustments easier when continuously welded rail is laid at temperatures above or below the mean.

7-4. Steel castings

Generally, the weldability of steel castings is comparable to that of wrought steels. Cast steels are usually welded in order to join one cast item to another or to a wrought steel item, and to repair defects in damaged castings. The weldability of steels is primarily a function of composition and heat treatment. Therefore, the procedures and precautions required for welding wrought steel also apply to cast steels of similar composition, heat treatment, and strength. Welding cast steels can sometimes be simplified by first considering the load in the area being welded and the actual strength needed in the weld. Castings are often complex; a specific analysis may be required only for part of the entire structure. When welding a section of steel casting that does not require the full strength of the casting, one can sometimes use lower-strength weld rods or wires, or the part being welded to the casting can be of lower strength and leaner analysis than the cast steel part. Under such conditions, the deposited weld metal usually has to match only the strength of the lower-strength member. With heat-treatable electrodes, the necessary welding sometimes can be done before final heat-treating. After being subjected to an austenitizing treatment (heating above the upper critical temperature), weld deposits with carbon contents less than 0.12 percent usually have lower mechanical properties than they have in the as-welded or stress-relieved condition.

a. *Weld joint design for structural welds.* Joint designs for cast steel weldments are similar to those used for wrought steel. AWS D1.1, Section 2 contains design criteria for welded connections and a list of prequalified joint designs. Any other type of joint design must be qualified before being used in the structure. When designing a welded connection, one should consider the type of weld process that will be used, the strength of the filler metal, and the welder's access to the joint,

b. *Recommended filler metals.* The choice of electrode filler metal is based on the type of cast steel being used, the strength needs of the joint, and the post-weld heat treatment. When welding carbon or low-alloy cast steels, the electrodes recommended for comparable wrought steel plate should be used, When cast austenitic stainless steels are joined to either cast or wrought ferritic materials, the proper filler metal depends on the service conditions. If the service temperature is low (below 600 °F) and the stresses are moderate, a high-alloy austenitic stainless steel, such as Type 309 or 310, is generally used. For service conditions under higher temperatures and stress, the high-nickel welding materials (70 percent Nickel-15 percent Chromium) are better because their thermal expansion is closer to that of the ferritic materials. High-nickel weld metal retards carbon migration; and this weld metal should be used with a technique to reduce nickel's dilution of the ferritic material.

7-5. Dissimilar combinations

Fabrication procedures often combine cast austenitic and ferritic steels, or cast austenitic materials and wrought ferritic materials. Each combination presents distinct problems. Dissimilar metals are often used for surfacing cast carbon steels. Here the problem is to select a process and technique causing minimum dilution. This insures freedom from underbead and weld cracking and improves the quality of the surfacing deposit. The proper techniques and materials are similar to those for wrought materials. AWS, sources of welding equipment, and metal suppliers can provide more information about the successful welding and satisfactory services of weldments of many of these combinations. Data not available from these sources may have to be obtained by testing.

7-6. Coated and clad materials

a. Composite materials. Composite materials are often used in structures to obtain special properties. Generally, a thick supporting layer of base metal is bonded to a thin layer of another metal, often more expensive, which has the desirable properties. These may include corrosion resistance, thermal or electrical conductivity, abrasion resistance, or decorative appeal. The composites may be obtained by

several processes, such as plating, cladding, lining, and weld overlay. When welding before coating, one must consider how the weld metal and coating metal can affect each other. For example, the welding operation may damage the coating, or the coating may adversely affect the weld. When welding cladplate and applied-liner construction, the operator must control the dilution of weld metal where the two metals meet. Joint penetration, electrode selection, welding process, and welding techniques are important considerations in welding clad materials and applied liners. Detailed information is in the AWS *Welding Handbook,* section 5.

b. Galvanized steel. When possible, welding should be done first, since galvanizing over welds is easy. Steel already galvanized can be welded with either the electric arc or gas welding processes, but the zinc coating next to the weld maybe damaged so much that it will not protect the steel. Thus, a coating must be applied to the welded joint to protect it from corrosion. The joint might be designed so that the galvanized steel is subjected to tensile stresses during welding or upon cooling. The stressed metal could fracture when the molten zinc or zinc vapor penetrates into the welded joint. Before welding, therefore, the zinc should be removed from all joints and surfaces of strength members. This should be done far enough from the expected toes of the weld to prevent such embrittlement. Light-gauge galvanized sheet metal may be welded by GMAW without substantially damaging the galvanized coating; this can be done with phosphor-bronze filler metal, or the carbon arc process can be used with or without silicon-bronze filler metal. More information on welding zinc-coated steel is in AWS D19.0.

CHAPTER 8

INSPECTION PROCEDURES

8-1. General

Weld joints are inspected for two reasons. First, inspection is used to determine the quality of specific joints and to insure this quality meets the applicable specifications. Weld defects are detected and their location noted, so the unacceptable part of the weld can be removed and replaced with sound weld metal. The second need for weld inspection is just as important but is less frequently recognized. Weld inspection serves as a quality control on the welding operators or welding procedures. Records of how often various types of defects occur can show when changes in welding procedures are needed, when poor welding practices are being used, or when the welders or welding operators should be requalified. A responsible fabricator will depend on inspection records to provide advance notice that the welding operations need attention. The fabricator will be able to correct problems soon enough to prevent the lost time and high costs of frequent repairs.

8-2. Qualification of personnel

Personnel doing nondestructive testing must be qualified according to the current requirements of the ASNT SNT-TC-1A. If applicable, nondestructive testing personnel can be certified under MIL-STD-410, or MIL-STD-271.

8-3. Inspectors

The inspector must uphold all quality criteria as defined in applicable specifications and standards and must judge whether the weldments inspected conform in all respects to the specifications. The inspector must know the limitations of the testing methods, the material, and the welding process. Ideally, the inspector also must have integrity and be willing to accept the responsibilities of the position.

8-4. Inspection

Virtually **every** inspection method available has been used to examine welds: visual, magnetic particle, liquid penetrant and ultrasonic, destructive, leak testing, and radiographic --- X-rays and radioisotopes. Acoustic emission and eddy current inspection have been used in production testing, but are not yet being used in field inspections. Table 8-1

lists the advantages and disadvantages of various inspection techniques. The method and extent of the inspection vary with the nature of the work and the criticality of certain joints. The following factors should be considered in selecting nondestructive test methods for weldments:

—Material to be tested.
—Joining process.
—Geometry of material.
—Possible or expected defects and their orientation,
—Economic considerations.

Some weldments may require combinations of two or more inspection methods to provide adequate evaluation. Questionable results from one method often may be verified by another method. Destructive testing is used primarily for the qualification of welding procedures , welders, welding operators, and sometimes for quality control.

a. Inspection procedures. The quality, integrity, properties, and dimensions of materials and components can be inspected with methods that do not cause damage. The following are nondestructive test methods:

—Visual inspection.
—Penetrant inspection.
—Magnetic particle inspection.
—Radiographic inspection.
—Ultrasonic inspection.
—Leak testing.

It is particularly important to inspect tank welds and root passes of multi-pass welds before more weld metal is deposited. These welds are thinner than the subsequent weld passes and therefore more likely to crack. If there is a crack, it may propagate with subsequent passes. If this happens, the entire weld must be removed and the joint rewelded. It is less expensive and quicker to replace defective tack welds and root passes before more weld metal is added. Thus, these welds should be inspected as soon as they are made. Follow-up inspection of root passes is important because subsequent passes may seal a crack so tightly that it cannot be detected by visual inspection. Inspection of the completed weld would indicate it is sound.

Table 8-1. Uses of Various Inspection Techniques

	Magnetic particle	Penetrant	Ultrasonic	X-ray
When to use	Suitable for detecting surface and subsurface flaws, cracks, porosity, nonmetallic inclusions, and weld defects.	Used to locate surface cracks, porosity, laps, cold shuts, lack of weld bond, fatigue, and grinding cracks.	Pulse-echo used to find internal defects, lack of bond, laminations, inclusions, porosity, grain structure; resonance used primarily for thickness gaging and laminar flaws.	Detection of internal flaws and detects; weld flaw detection includes cracks, seams, porosity, holes, and inclusions, checking assemblies, lack of bond, and thickness variations.
Where to use	Used on all types of ferro-magnetic materials—tubing, piping of any size, shape, compposition or state of heat-treatment; used for in-service testing for fatigue cracks.	Used on all metals, glass, ceramics, cast-ings, forgings, machined parts, cutting tools, and for field inspection.	Used on all metals and hard nonmetallic materials—sheets, tubes, rods, forg-ings, castings—in field and production testing. In-service part testing for aircraft and marine inspection.	Used on forgings, castings, tubing, formed metal parts, welded vessels; used in field testing of welds, corrosion surveys, and assemblies.
Reasons to use	Simple in principle. easy to perform, portable for field testing, fast for production testing; method is positive and cost is economical.	Simple to apply, accurate, fast, low initial cost and per test copy, easy to interpret results, no elaborate set-up required.	Fast and dependable, easy to operate. Lends itself to automation, results of test immediately known, relative-ly portable, highly accurate and sensitive.	Provides permanent record on film, better on thin sections; often higher sensitivity, fluoroscopy techniques available with adjustable energy level.
Limita-tions	Parts must be magnetic; requires demagnetizing after tests. Power source is needed, and parts must be cleaned before finishing.	Limited to surface defects; surface cleanli-ness required.	Requires contact or immersion of part to be tested; interpretation of defects requires training.	Higher initial cost, power source required, radiation hazard; trained technicians required.

b. Repair of defective welds. When a defective weld is removed and the joint rewelded, the repair weld should be inspected in the same way as the original weld. The surfaces of the joint from which the defective metal was removed should be inspected to make sure the defect is completely gone. Cracks should be checked very carefully. If part of a crack is allowed to remain, it may propa-gate through a repair weld; this must be avoided. A series of inspections and metal removals may be needed.

8-5. Visual inspection

Visual inspection, which is the most widely used inspection method, is also the quickest, easiest, and cheapest. The only equipment commonly used is a magnifying glass (1 OX or less) and a flashlight or extension. Other tools, such as a borescope and den-tal mirrors, are useful for inspection inside vessels, pipe, or confined areas. Visual inspection is always required in weld evaluation. However, it will not reveal interval defects or minute surface defects.

a. Examination prior to welding. Before welding, the faces and edges should be examined for lamina-tions, blisters, scabs, and seams. Heavy scale, oxide films, grease, paint, oil, and dirt should be removed.

Edge preparation, alignment of parts, and fit-up should be checked. Welding specifications should be specific and state that all weld joints must be inspected for compliance with requirements for preparation, placement of consumable inserts, align-ment, fit-up, and cleanliness.

b. Examination of welds during welding. Specifi-cations should state that welds must be examined for conformance to the qualified welding procedure, detection of cracks in root pass, weld bead thick-ness, slag and flux removal, and preheat and interpass temperatures, where applicable.

c. Examination of welds after welding. Specifica-tions should state that welds must 'be examined for cracks, contour and finish, bead reinforcement, undercutting, overlap, and size of fillet welds. A weld is considered acceptable by visual inspection if:

(1) The weld has no surface flaws such as cracks, porosity, unfilled craters, and crater cracks, particu-larly at the end of welds.

(2) The weld metal and base metal are fused. The edges of the weld metal should blend smoothly and gradually into the adjacent base metal. There should be no unacceptable overlap or undercut.

(3) The weld profiles conform to   referenced standards and specifications. The faces of fillet welds may be slightly convex, flat, or slightly concave, as determined by use of suitable gages or templates (fig 8-1). The minimum size of each fillet leg is specified on the applicable drawings or welding procedure. For butt welds, the amount of weld bead reinforcement or the height of the surface of the weld above the base metal surface should be no greater than the welding specification allows (fig 8-2). (These standards should be developed early in a job, and should represent acceptable, borderline, and rejectable conditions. When there are several critical   joints, a separate standard may be prepared for each.) The objective of all inspection methods is to reveal any flaws or defects that may affect a part's service performance. Therefore, a joint should be cleaned to remove anything that would hinder inspection; e.g., slag and oxide films. Care should be taken when a cleaning method such as shot-blasting is used. Fine cracks and similar imperfections may be sealed on the surface and made invisible. In visual inspection, it is essential to correctly interpret and evaluate discrepancies in the appearance of welds. Thus, the inspector needs to understand the welding process in order to evaluate the quality of a weld.

8-6. Magnetic particle inspection

Magnetic particle inspection is a nondestructive method of detecting cracks, seams, inclusions, segregations, porosity, lack of fusion, and similar flaws in ferromagnetic materials such as steels and some stainless steel   alloys.   This method of inspection can detect discontinuities which may be too fine to be seen with the naked eye; it can also detect some subsurface defects, depending on the depth of flaw

and type of inspection current used. Magnetic particle inspection is advantageous because it can be used on any magnetic material and is a rapid, inexpensive, and very reliable method when used by trained inspectors. The main disadvantage is that it applies only to magnetic materials and is not suited for very small, deep-seated defects. The deeper the defect is, the larger it must be for detection. Subsurface defects are easier to find when they have a crack-like shape, such as lack of fusion   in welds. Welds with rough surfaces may present difficulties. The process' sensitivity is decreased by this roughness, which mechanically interferes with the pattern formed by iron oxide particles (see a below).

a. Principles of magnetic particle inspection. The part to be inspected is magnetized by passing through it a low-voltage, high-amperage electric current, or by placing it in a magnetic field. Any discontinuities such as cracks or lack of fusion disrupt the magnetic field that has been established. Electrical poles form at the ends of the flaws (fig 8-3). Fine magnetic particles applied to the surface of the part are attracted to these electrical poles. The concentration of particles can be seen and the flaw located.

(1) The ease with which a magnetic flux can be developed in a material is known as its permeability. The property of any magnetic material to keep or retain a magnetic field after the magnetizing current is removed is called retentivity. Metals which lose most of their magnetism as soon as the magnetizing current is removed have low retentivity. Usually a magnetized metal that has high permeability has low retentivity, while a metal with a low permeability has high retentivity. Construction steels generally have low retentivity.

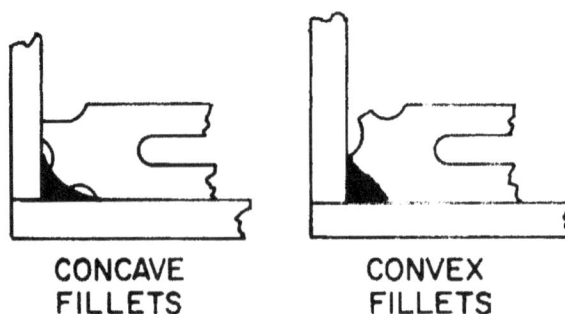

CONCAVE FILLETS   CONVEX FILLETS

U.S. Army Corps of Engineers

Figure 8-1. Gages for measuring fillet weld contour

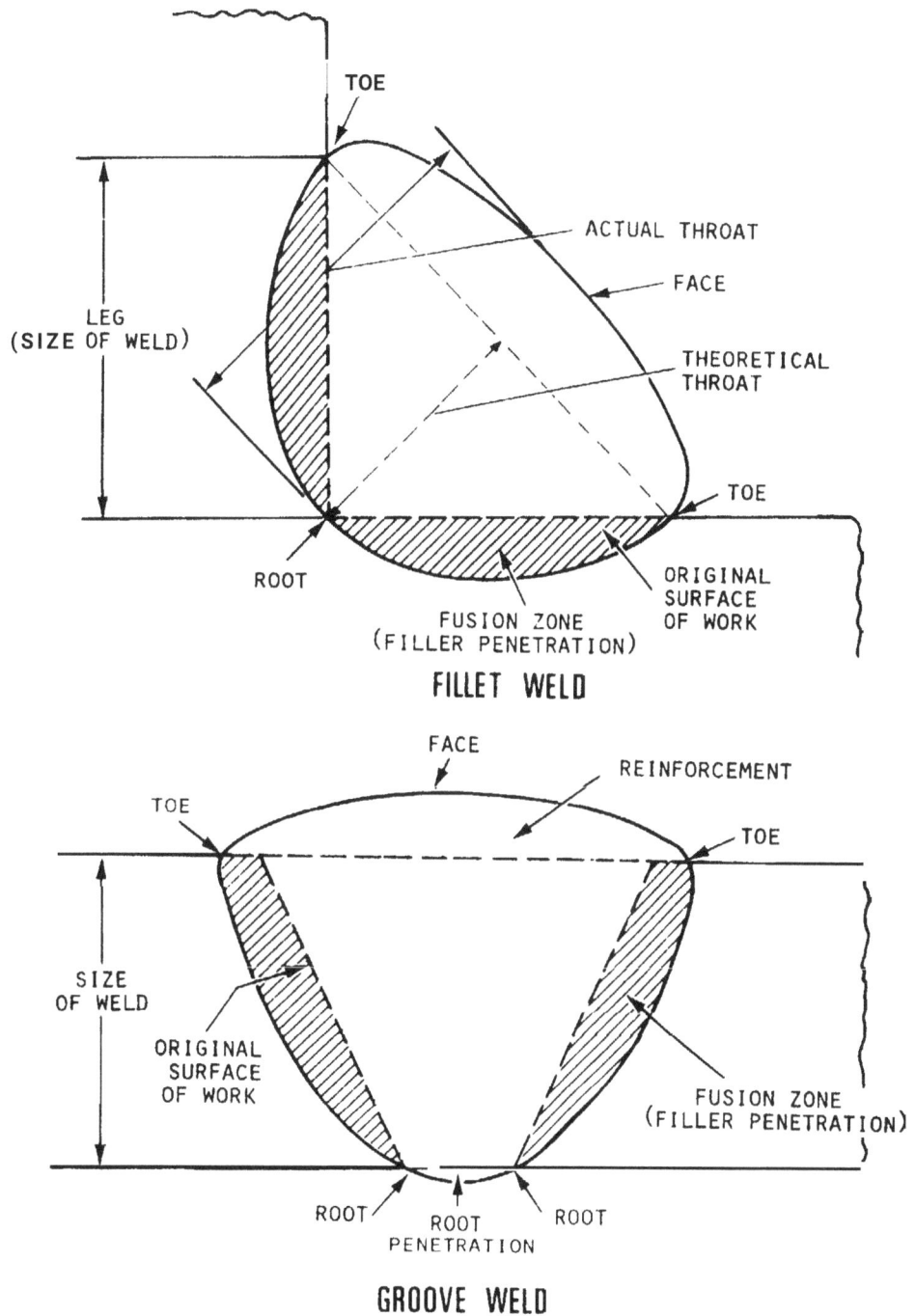

FILLET WELD

GROOVE WELD

Reprinted from TM 9-237, Welding Theory
and Application, Department of the Army,
1976 (noncopyrighted).

Figure 8-2. Weld nomenclature.

MAGNETIC LINES
OF FORCE

A. SOUND WELD

MAGNETIC PARTICLE
INDICATION

B. CRACKED WELD

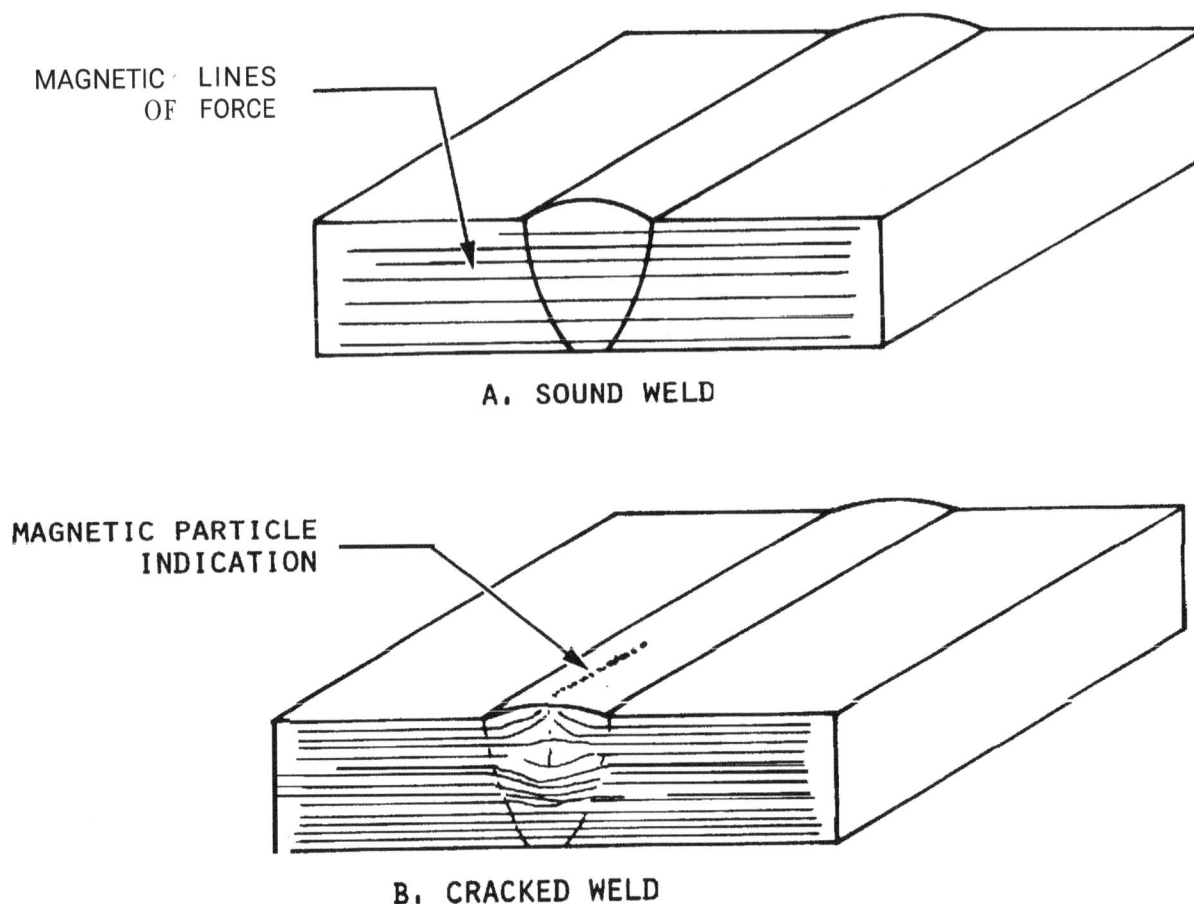

Reprinted from TM 5-805-7, Welding Design,
Procedures and Inspection, Department of
the Army, 1968 (noncopyrighted).

Figure 8-3. Disruption of magnetic field by weld-metal defect

(2) DC, AC, and half-wave rectified current may be used for magnetization. High-amperage, low-voltage current is usually employed. If only surface defects are to reinspected, AC can be used. DC isused for the detection of subsurface discontinuities because the current penetrates throughout the part. Maximum sensitivity is provided by using half-wave rectified, single-phase current. The pulsating field increases the particle mobility and enables the particles to lineup more readily in weak leakage fields. The pulse peaks also produce a higher magnetizing force, which is needed in the inspection of welds.

(3) The magnetic particles may be applied to the weld either as a dry powder or as a suspension in a light oil. The particles used are carefully selected iron oxide particles of the proper size, shape, magnetic permeability, and retentivity. Dry particles are in powder form and may be obtained in gray, red, or black for contrast. These particles are applied using hand shakers, spray bulbs, shaking screens, or an airstream. Wet particles consist of particles suspended in a light petroleum oil or kerosene. They can be applied   b y dipping, immersing, or spraying from aerosol cans.   The particles can be colored or

have a fluorescent coating for viewing with ultraviolet light. Wet particles provide better control and standardization of the concentration of magnetic particles through control of the concentration of suspension. The wet procedure is more sensitive for the detection of extremely small discontinuities below the surface. Excess powder should be removed with a stream of air of just enough force to carry the excess away without disturbing lightly held powder patterns.

(4) A method of applying the bath or particles after the magnetizing current has been turned off is called the "residual method. " This method of applying the particles is effective on materials that will retain their magnetism, i.e., those having high retentivity. Steel that is relatively high in carbon and other alloys responds most favorably to this method. Most construction steels, however, have low retentivity and will not hold a strong enough magnetic field for this method. The recommended method for construction steels is the "continuous method"; magnetizing is done at the same time the inspection medium or particles are applied. This method is particularly useful when inspecting low carbon or alloy steels. Because of their low retentivity, the parts cannot maintain enough residual magnetism to hold the particles needed to indicate a defect. Whether wet or dry continuous methods are used, the inspector must be careful not to wash or shake off the magnetic particle indications. Excessive current must not be used during magnetizing because this may produce irrelevant indications. Because of the strong field produced, the continuous method is especially useful in locating subsurface defects.

(5) When current is passed through a coil which is wrapped around a material, a magnetic field is produced in that material. This is called longitudinal magnetization. When clamps or prods are used to pass the current through the material, the procedure is called circular magnetization. The two methods produce magnetic fields in different directions, thereby permitting the inspector to examine a material for discontinuities in all directions.

b. Equipment. Various types of magnetizing equipment are available. Units with electromagnets and permanent magnets are commonly used, but are designed for locating surface cracks. Although such a unit can locate some subsurface defects, its depth of penetration is severely limited. Direct current equipment provides the great depth of penetration needed to detect subsurface flaws. Some equipment has both full-wave and half-wave rectified direct current (HWDC). HWDC is particularly suitable for use with dry particles because the pulsating field provides excellent mobility to the powder particles,

Since most construction steels have low retentivity, demagnetization is generally not required; however, most magnetic particle inspection units can demagnetize after inspection.

c. Inspection procedures. The procedures decribed substantially conform to ASTM E 138 and ASTM E 709. MIL-I-6868 and the ASME Boiler and Pressure Vessel Code, section V, also outline inspection procedures. The surface of the weld usually does not require grinding or smoothing before testing. However, if the edges of the weld are undercut or-if the bead surface is extremely rough, the weld should be ground smooth and the edges blended into the base metal surface before magnetic particle inspection. The surface should be cleaned of all grease, oil, loose rust, or water because such materials interfere with the particles which indicate defects.

(1) The "prod method" of weld inspection is widely used. Portable prod-type electrical contacts are pressed against the surface of the material next to the weld, as shown in figure 8-4. The prods should not be spaced more than 8 inches apart. A shorter prod spacing with a minimum of 3 inches may be used to increase sensitivity. When the prods are positioned, the operator turns the current on and applies the magnetic particle powders. The current is turned off before the prods are removed in order to prevent arcing. At least two separate examinations should be done for each area. The prods are repositioned so that the lines of flux from one operation are approximately perpendicular to the lines of flux from the previous operation. Contact clamps sometimes can be used instead of prods.

(2) The weld must be examined immediately after the excess powder has been removed and before the position of the prods is changed. Surface defects appear as sharp indications, while subsurface indications are broad, diffuse patterns.

(3) Acceptance standards are written based on the object's intended use. Standards vary, but most specify similar limits for possible defects.

8-7. Penetrant inspection

Penetrant inspection is a sensitive, nondestructive method of locating minute flaws open to the surface — for example, cracks, pores, and leaks. It is particularly valuable for examining nonmagnetic materials, on which magnetic particle inspection cannot be used. Penetrant inspection is used extensively for exposing surface defects in aluminum, magnesium, and austenitic stainless steel weldments, and for locating leaks in all welds. Dye penetrant procedures usually require ground surfaces, although some "as-welded" surfaces can be inspected.

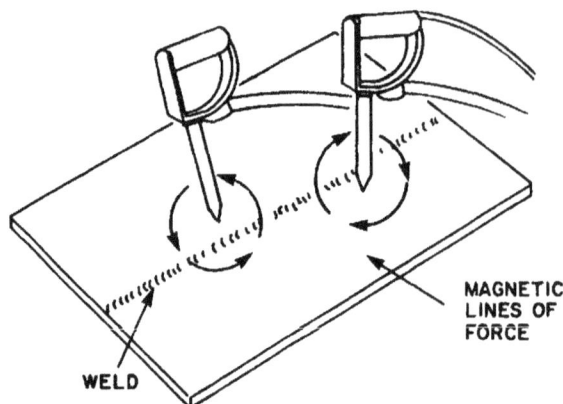

Figure 8-4. Magnetic field created around a weld as current is passed between two test prods.

(Improper grinding can smear the surface and close surface openings of the defects.) The efficiency of the method depends on the inspector's ability to recognize and evaluate the visual indications of flaws.

a. Principles of liquid penetrant inspection. In liquid penetrant inspection, both visible and fluorescent, the surface of a material is coated with a film of penetrating liquid (fig 8-5). The liquid is allowed to seep into any flaws that are open to the surface, and the excess surface film is removed. A developer is then applied; it draws the penetrant from a discontinuity to the surface so the inspector can see the flaw.

(1) Liquid penetrant inspection can be done quickly and easily; it costs less per foot of weld inspected than any other nondestructive method except visual inspection. The initial cost of training, equipment, materials, and supplies is much less than that of any other inspection method. However, surface porosity and improper surface cleanliness reduce the sensitivity of the inspection technique; contaminants such as water, oil, and grease can cover or fill discontinuities so the penetrant does not enter. Penetrant inspection methods are used to check nonporous materials for defects open to the surface. The following surface defects can be found with penetrant inspection: all types of cracks in connection with welding, grinding, fatigue, forging, etc.; porosity; seams; laps; cold shuts; or lack of bond between two metals. Since penetrant methods can locate only surface defects, cleanliness is extremely important.

(2) penetrant inspection is equally applicable to both large and small weldments. In the petrochemical industries, pressure vessels and piping, which are often made of nonmagnetic materials, can be inspected for surface cracks and porosity by this method. Penetrant inspection can be used to detect cracks, pores, and leaks through the lining in clad vessels. This method can be applied to all types of welded linings. Shallow cracks and porosity can be distinguished from those that extend through the lining (leakers). The indications for all cracks and porosity bleed out rapidly or spread upon application of dry developer.

b. Equipment. The equipment used in penetrant inspection is portable: aerosol cans of cleaner, dye, and developer. When fluorescent penetrant is used, a black light source in the 36-angstrom unit range and a hood or dark area are required. Portable inspection kits for field use are commercially available.

Inspection procedures. The procedure described substantially conforms to ASTM E 165.

(1) Either the visible or fluorescent dye penetrant method can be used between a series of stringer welds or on a completed weld. There are three types of penetrant: water washable, post emulsifying, and solvent removable. Intermixing these penetrant materials is not permitted. Procedures for inspection depend on the specific type of penetrant and the method used; therefore, only a general approach is outlined in this manual.

PENETRATION	WASH	DEVELOPMENT	INSPECTION
FLUORESCENT PENETRANT ON SURFACE SEEPS INTO CRACKS	WATER SPRAY REMOVES PENETRANT FROM SURFACE BUT NOT FROM CRACKS AND PORES	DEVELOPER ACTS LIKE A BLOTTER TO DRAW PENETRANT OUT OF CRACK	BLACK LIGHT CAUSES PENETRANT TO GLOW IN DARK

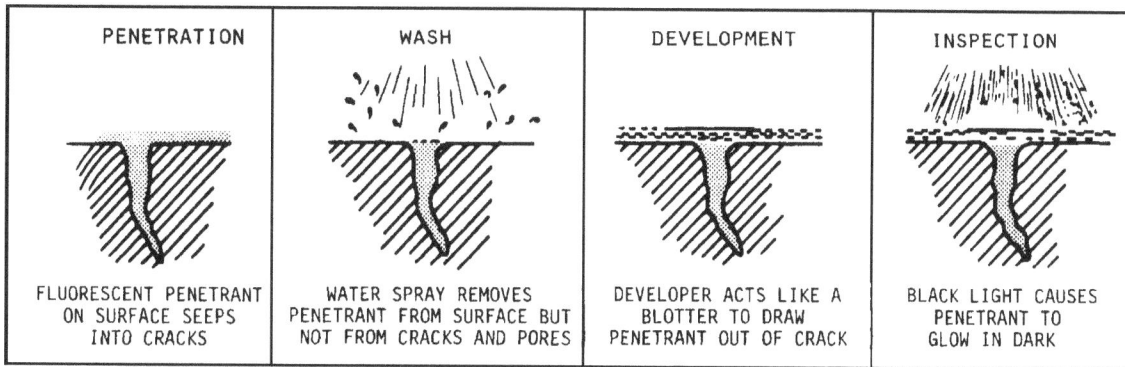

Reprinted from AF Study Guide ABR 53630-201 (noncopyrighted).

Figure 8-5. Major steps of fluorescent penetrant inspection.

(2) The surface must be clean and dry. The discontinuity must be free of oil, water, or other contaminants so that the void is open and the penetrant can enter. The method of cleaning the weld area is unimportant part of the test procedure.

(3) The penetrant is applied to the surface by spraying or brushing. The inspector must allow enough time for the penetrant to enter all discontinuities. A minimum time of 10 minutes at a temperature of 60 to 125 degrees F is normally recommended. The smaller the defect or the higher the sensitivity required, the longer the penetrating time must be.

(4) Excess penetrant can be removed from the surface by wiping with an absorbent cloth, either dry or moistened with a solvent. Removing the surface penetrant by spraying with solvents gives a clean surface; however, penetrant can be washed out of defects if the spraying is not done very carefully. Therefore, this technique is not recommended.

(5) The developer should be applied carefully so it does not produce a coat so thick that indications are masked. The developer acts as a blotter to draw the penetrant to the surface, where it can be seen with the naked eye or viewed under an ultraviolet light (in fluorescent penetrant inspection). The developer must be applied as soon as possible after the penetrant removal operation; the time between the application of the developer and interpretation should be controlled ((6) below). The true size and type of defect are difficult to appraise if the dye diffuses too much in the developer. The recommended practice is to observe the surface during the application of the developer in order to see certain indications which might tend to bleed out quickly.

(6) Interpretation must be done within a specified time. The specification might indicate, for example, that interpretation must be done no sooner than 7 minutes and no later than 30 minutes after application of the developer.

(7) Most acceptance standards specify similar limits on cracks and linear indications, rounded indications of a specific size and quantity, or number of indications in a given area.

8-8. Radiographic inspection

Radiographic inspection is a nondestructive testing technique which involves taking a picture of the internal condition of a material. This picture is produced by directing a beam of short wave-length radiation (X-rays or gamma rays) through a material that would be opaque to ordinary light. This radiation exposes a film which is placed on the opposite side of the material. When developed, the film (called a radiograph) shows the presence or absence of internal defects. Radiographic inspection is called for in many specifications because it provides a permanent record. Different types of internal defects can be identified, and flaws such as cracks, porosity, lack of fusion, and entrapped slag can be differentiated. Radiographic inspection has its limitations, however. These include high initial cost, radiation hazards, the need for highly trained technicians, and the requirement that certain defects, particularly cracks and lack of fusion, be correctly oriented with respect to the beam of radiation (if the orientation is incorrect, the defects will not be recorded on the film).

a. Principles of radiographic inspection. Radiography uses the penetrating power of radiation to reveal the interior of a material. Radiation from a source passes through an object and causes a change in the film emulsion when the film is developed. The amount of darkening of the film, referred to as density, depends on the amount of film exposure caused by radiation penetrating the thick or thin sections of the object. The procedure for radiographic testing is

shown schematically in figure 8-6. The cone of radiation could also represent a gamma-ray capsule containing radioactive material such as those listed in table 8-2. Not all of the radiation penetrates the weld. Some is absorbed, the amount depending on the density and thickness of the weld and on the material being inspected. A cavity, such as a blowhole in the weld interior, leaves less metal for the radiation to pass through, so that the amount absorbed by the weld will vary in the defective region. These variations, if measured or recorded on a radiation-sensitive film, produce an image that will indicate the presence of the defect. In applying radiographic inspection, care is required to insure that the procedure is carried out properly. Inadequate technique can result in poor sensitivity, irrelevant indications, or other problems.

Table 8-2. Characteristics of Radioisotope Sources

	Cobalt Co-60	Radium Ra-226	Cesium Ce-137	Iridium Ir-192	Thulium Tm-170
Radiation level, RHF/curie*	14.5	9.0	4.2	5.9	0.03
Half-life, years	5.3	1600	30	75	130
Half-value layer (lead), in.	0.5	0.5	0.3	0.2	0.05
Energy (MeV)	1.25	1.22	0.66	0.355	0.072
X-ray equivalent** (MeV)	2 to 3	1 to 2	0.6 to 1.5	0.3 to 0.8	0.1 to 0.3

* RHF = roentgen-hr-ft.
**X-ray equivalent is the approximate X-ray energy required to provide the same penetrations as the isotope.

b. Equipment. The equipment required for radiographic inspection is either an X-ray machine or gamma source, film, penetrameters, film developing equipment, and viewing equipment, as described below. In ASTM E 94, the table "Type of Industrial Radiographic Film" lists film characteristics; the table "Guide for Selection of Film" lists recommendations for radiation sources and film types to be used with a variety of alloys in different section thicknesses.

(1) X-ray machines are available in a wide range of sizes and voltage ratings. The kilovoltage rating required depends on the thickness and type of metal to be radiographed.

(2) Radioactive sources and x-radiation have similar effects on radiation-sensitive film. The difference between the rays is the origin. X-ray radiation is generated in an X-ray tube, while gamma radiation is emitted from a radioactive isotope. Table 8-2 gives some of the more important characteristics of radioisotopes. These figures are rough estimates, but do show the relative positions of the sources in order of their energy.

(3) Gamma radiography is used frequently in construction work because no external power is required, which makes it suitable for inspection in remote areas; the cost of the equipment and source is much less than that of X-ray equipment with a comparable kilovolt range; the isotope equipment is more easily transported; the equipment is rugged

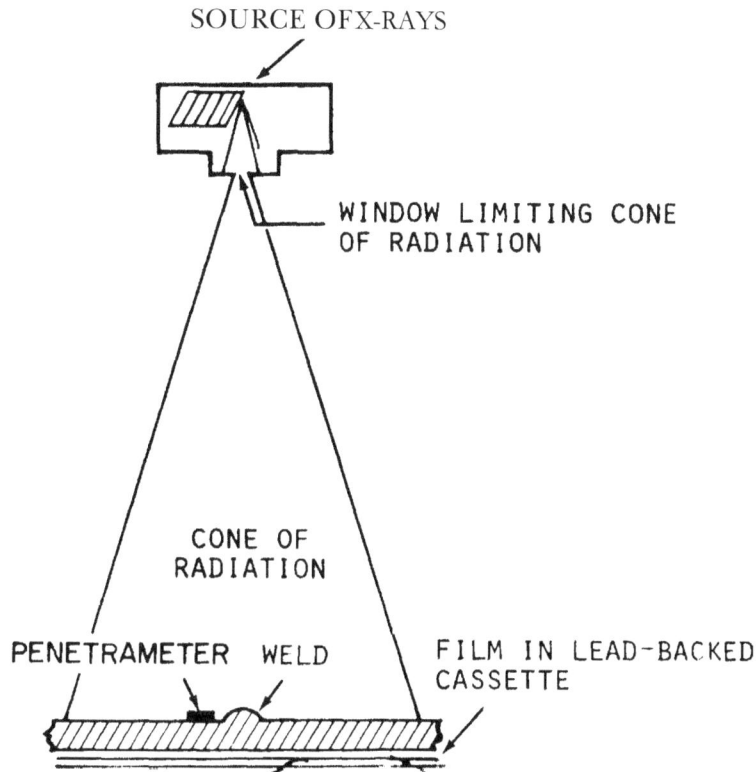

SOURCE OF X-RAYS

WINDOW LIMITING CONE
OF RADIATION

CONE OF
RADIATION

PENETRAMETER   WELD   FILM IN LEAD-BACKED
CASSETTE

Reprinted from MIL HDBK 58, Thermal
Joining of Metals, Processes Other Than
Arc Welding, Department of Defense, 1971
(noncopyrighted).

Figure 8-6. Radiographic setup.

and simple to operate and maintain; and confined spaces can reinspected because of the small source size. However, there are several disadvantages to isotope sources. Among these is a severe radiation hazard. These sources must be stored in locked, shielded cases, and handled very carefully when used. Personnel performing radiography must be highly trained and must relicensed by the Nuclear Regulatory Commission. The radiographs generally have considerably less contrast than films exposed by X-radiation. The cost and trouble of replacing isotopes with short half-lives can be a factor in deciding whether to use X-ray or gamma radiography on a project.

(4) The image quality of a radiograph can be shown by using a penetrameter. This is a piece of metal similar to that being inspected. It is placed near the weld on the source side during radiography to determine the degree of sensitivity disclosed in a radiograph. For example, if a penetrameter with a thickness of 2 percent of the material to be inspected can be seen on the radiograph, it means that the radiograph contrast sensitivity is 2 percent or better, since the radiographic technique employed can show an object thickness difference of 2 percent or more. In most cases, 2 percent contrast sensitivity is considered satisfactory. However, for critical purposes such as nuclear components, pressure vessels, and piping for compressed gasses and

ALL DIMENSIONS IN INCHES

T= THICKNESS OF THE PENETRAMETER (LESS THAN 2% OF TEST SAMPLE THICKNESS)

{ DIAMETER = 2T BUT NOT LESS THAN 0.020"

DIAMETER = 1T BUT NOT LESS THAN 0.010"

DIAMETER = 4T BUT NOT LESS THAN 0.040"

{ IDENTIFICATION NUMBER SHOWING MINIMUM THICKNESS ON WHICH THE PENETRAMETER MAY BE USED. NUMBER MUST SHOW IN RADIOGRAPH.

ALL HOLES SHALL BE TRUE AND NORMAL TO THE SURFACE AND NOT CHAMFERED.

PENETRAMETERS SHALL BE MADE OF MATERIAL BEING TESTED.

PENETRAMETER THICKNESSES EXCEEDING 2-1/2

PENETRAMETER FOR THICKNESS NOT GREATER THAN 2-1/2

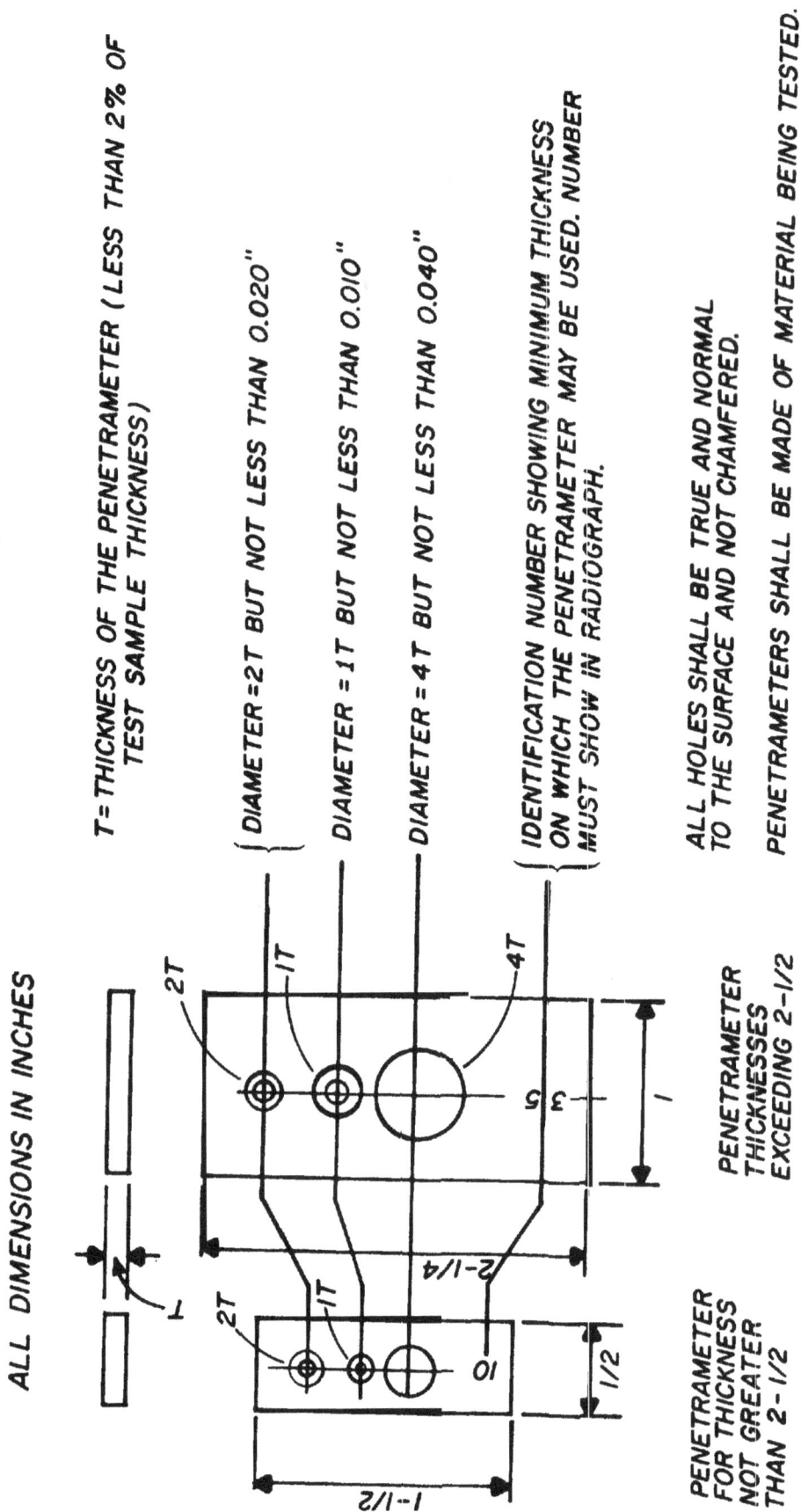

Reprinted from MIL HDBK 55, Radiography Nondestructive Testing, Department of Defense, 1968 (noncopyrighted).

Figure 8-7. Details of penetrameters.

bridges, a lower percentage is desired. In other classes of work, a higher percentage maybe acceptable. To demonstrate detail sensitivity, holes in the penetrameter are used; their diameters are, in terms of effect, artificial flaws of known dimensions. The holes are usually expressed in the thickness of the penetrameter. Construction details of penetrameters are shown in figure 8-7.

(5) The radiographic film must be Class 1, extra fine grain, and Class 2, fine grain. Both classes of film give high contrast. Extra fine grain film has greater sensitivity than fine grain (i.e., reveal smaller discontinuities). However, exposure times may be as much as 50 percent longer since more exposure to radiation is needed to develop an image. Film holders must be flexible, and intensification screens must be made of lead. Front screens should be 0.005 inch and back screens 0.010 inch.

(6) Film processing equipment can be either manual or automatic. Processing systems should contain separate tanks for developing, short stop or washing, fixing, and final washing. Film driers must not cause processing defects.

(7) A densitometer or a density strip is needed to make sure film density requirements have been met. Density, a measure of the degree of blackness, is a function of exposure time and intensity of the radiation to which film is subjected. The radiographer controls these variables.

c. Inspection procedure. The procedure described substantially conforms to ASTM E 94, ASTM E 142, and AWS D1.1. Procedures are also outlined in MIL-R-11470, MIL-STD-453, and the ASME Boiler and Pressure Vessel Code, section V.

(1) Radiographs must be made by either the X-ray or isotope radiation methods. If the level 2-2T radiography is required, all radiographs should reveal discontinuities with thicknesses equal to or greater than 2 percent of the thickness of the thinner part joined by the weld being examined. In the "2-2T" designation, the first digit 2 means 2 percent sensitivity and 2T the diameter of the hole in the penetrameter which must be clearly visible in the radiograph. Class 1 or 2 film must be used. The film must be clean and free of processing defects. It must have a density of not less than 1.5 nor more than 4.0, although densities within the range of 2.5 to 3.5 are preferred. Radiographs will show:

(a) The smallest hole in each penetrameter as specified in the specification.

(b) The radiograph identification and location.

(2) Welds that are to be radiographed need not be ground or otherwise smoothed for radiographic testing unless the surface irregularities interfere with the desired radiographic image. When weld reinforcement or backing is not removed, shims of the material being radiographed must be placed _ under the penetrameter. These shims must make the total thickness of material between the penetrameter and the film at least equal to the average thickness of the weld measured through its reinforcement and backing.

(3 Pnetrameters must be placed on the side of the work near the radiation source adjacent and parallel to the weld, A radiograph identification mark and two location identification marks, all of which are to show in the radiograph, must be placed on the material at each radiograph location.

(4) Film holders must be placed tightly against the test item whenever possible. Shielding beyond the film holder should be provided when practical. The operator must use radiation detection devices, including survey meters, film badges, and dosimeters.

(5) Film must be processed so that the radiographs are of high quality. Films containing mechanical, chemical, or other processing defects that could interfere with proper interpretation of the radiograph are not acceptable.

(6) Radiographs are viewed using a high-intensity light source that has adjustable levels from dim to a brightness that penetrates without difficulty radiographs with a density of 4.0. Radiographs must be checked for proper placement of identification numbers and penetrameters. All indications must be interpreted and marked.

(7) The interpreter must be familiar with the standards for acceptance or rejection. Most standards agree about the types of discontinuities which are not acceptable, but there are some differences. Defects such as cracks or zones of incomplete fusion or penetration would be cause for rejection. Porosity of one size or aggregate lengths might also be cause for rejection, while other sizes or lengths would be acceptable. Reference radiographs are indicated in ASTM E 94, MIL-STD-779, and MIL-R-45774.

8-9. Ultrasonic inspection

Ultrasonic inspection is a rapid, efficient, nondestructive method of detecting, locating, and measuring both surface and subsurface defects in weldments and/or base materials. An ultrasonic is an energy wave form with frequencies above 20,000 Hertz. The ultrasonic wave is introduced into the material being tested by a piezoelectric transducer placed in contact with the test specimen. The ultrasound enters the specimen and is reflected back to the transducer when it encounters an interface that

Table 8-3. Comparison of Ultrasonics With Other Techniques

Radiography	Magnetic particle	Liquid penetrant	Ultrasonic
1. Porosity	1. All surface cracks	1. All surface cracks	1. Longitudinal cracks
2. Inclusions	2. Large slag	2. Porosity	2. Transverse cracks
3. Large cracks	3. Lack of penetration		3. Lack of fusion
4. Lack of fusion	4. Lack of fusion		4. Large slag
5. Lack of penetration	5. Subsurface cracks		5. Lack of penetration
6. Small cracks			6. Shallow surface cracks
			7. Small inclusions
			8. Porosity

Note: Listed in the order of ease of detection by each method.

could be a flaw or the back surface of the material. These vibrations are converted to electric signals, amplified, and displayed on a cathode ray tube (CRT) screen as indications. Because of the high frequency (above the range for the human ear), the short wave-length allows small flaws to be detected. Ultrasonics is one of the most commonly used techniques for subsurface flaw detection in weldments. Ultrasonic inspection is specified to detect both internal and surface flaws in all types of welded joints. Defects such as slag inclusions, porosity, lack of fusion (cold shuts), lack of penetration (root defects), and longitudinal and transverse cracks can be detected. Since only one inspection surface is usually required, many types of welded joints can be satisfactorily inspected. When a flaw is found, it can be measured and evaluated. Dimensions such as depth, width, and length can be measured if one surface is accessible.

a. Principles of ultrasonic inspection. Most ultrasonic testing is performed with a single straight or angle beam transducer depending on the design of the weld joint to be inspected. The transducer, sometimes referred to as a crystal or search unit, can transform electrical voltage generated by the ultrasonic unit into mechanical vibrations or ultrasound. The transducer also can convert the returning vibrations from a test specimen into electrical energy; they are displayed in this form on the ultrasonic unit's CRT. This capability to convert from electrical energy to mechanical vibrations and back again is called the piezoelectric effect. The electrical signal striking the transducer, usually not more than 1 microsecond in duration, makes the transducer vibrate during the driving period. The duration of the pulse is short, so that returning or reflected echoes from defects or boundaries lying close to the surface will appear as a separate indication, as shown in figure 8-8. Such a presentation is

called an A-scan and is a "time versus amplitude display." From the pip or pulse location on the CRT time line and its height of amplitude, the relative depth and size of the discontinuity can be estimated.

(1) Ultrasonic inspection has many advantages over other methods. It is fast, and the equipment is compact and portable. Unlike radiographic inspection, it involves no time delay while film is being processed and poses no radiation hazard to persons working in the inspection area. Indications of flaws can be seen immediately on the CRT. Both internal and surface flaws can be detected (though shallow surface cracks are more easily and reliably detected with magnetic particle or liquid penetrant). Since there are no expandable materials, the inspection can be performed faster and at a lower cost than radiography. Certain types of defects not readily detectable by other inspection methods can be found by ultrasonics. By using calibrated standards and a few calculations, the inspector can classify he indications as irrelevant, acceptable, or unacceptable. Ultrasonic inspection has a higher sensitivity level than does radiographic inspection. Ultrasonic inspection is more sensitive to crack detection as the material thickness increases; for radiographic inspection, the opposite is true. Table 8-3 compares ultrasonics and radiographic, magnetic particle, and liquid penetrant inspection.

(2) Ultrasonic inspection has some limitations that have restricted its use. Chief among these are the difficulty in interpreting the oscilloscope patterns and the need for standards to calibrate the instrument. This procedure produces no permanent records showing flaws and their location. A high degree of operator skill and training is required to interpret the oscilloscope patterns reliably. Flaws, such as cracks, oriented parallel to the sound beam may not be detected. This means a different ultrasonic inspection technique must be used. The

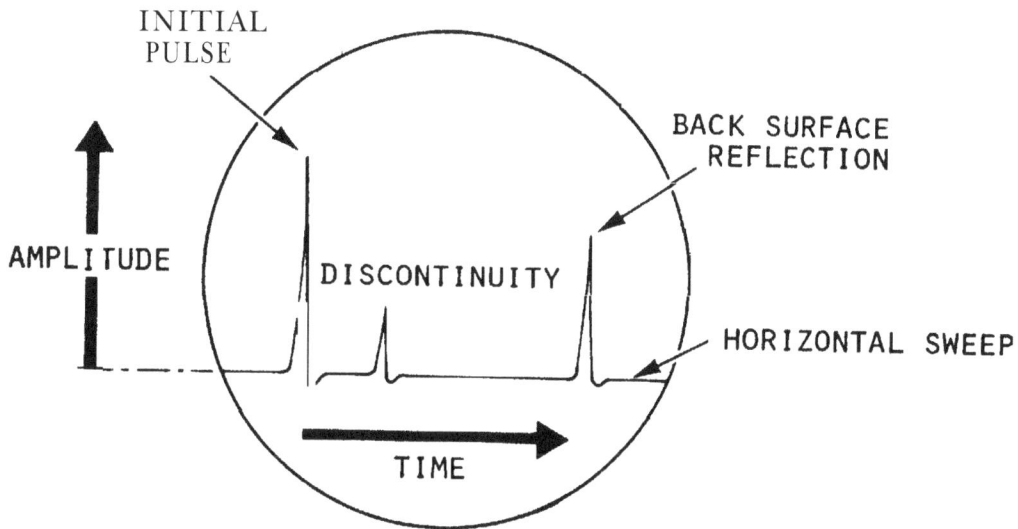

Reprinted from MIL HDBK 333 (USAF), Handbook for Standardization of Nondestructive Testing Methods, Department of Defense, 1974 (non-copyrighted).

Figure 8-8. A scan presentation on cathode ray tube

Table 8-4. Frequency-Application Chart

Frequency range	Test applications
200 kHz – 1 MHz	Castings: gray iron, nodular iron, and relatively coarse-grained materials, such as copper and stainless steels.
400 kHz – 5 MHz	Castings: steel, aluminum, brass, and other materials with refined grain size.
200 kHz – 2.25 MHz	Plastics and plastic-like materials, such as solid rocket propellants and powder grains.
1–5 MHz	Rolled products: metallic sheet, plate, bars, and billets.
2.25–10 MHz	Drawn and extruded products: bars, tubes, and shapes.
1–10 MHz	Forgings.
2.25–10 MHz	Glass and ceramics.
1–2.25 MHz	Welds.
1–10 MHz	Maintenance inspection, especially fatigue cracks.

surface of the material must be free from weld spatter and must be smooth enough to allow effective coupling between the transducer and the material. Surface roughness can cause scattering and absorption of the sound. Also, a rough surface will create undue wear on the crystal surface of the transducer, causing premature failure. A viscous coupling agent such as glycerine is necessary to eliminate the compressible air which prevents sound (mechanical vibrations) from entering the material from the transducer. The coupling agent can be any liquid, grease, or paste which fills surface depressions or pits.

(3) Two important considerations in selecting a transducer are its diameter and operating frequency. The higher the frequency, the greater the sensitivity will be. This advantage may be offset if lower frequencies are needed to penetrate coarse-grained or very thick materials. Table 8-4 shows the ultrasonic frequency ranges that may be used on various applications.

(4) Transducers generally fall into three groups: straight beam, angle beam, and surface wave.

(a) Longitudinal wave, sometimes called straight beam, directs the sound waves into the material in a direction perpendicular to the surface of the part. This method is used mainly to detect subsurface defects in base metals, but should be specified for some weld inspection, as shown in figure 8-9.

(b) The angle beam method, sometimes called shear wave, is usually the required procedure for weld inspection. The vibrational wave is introduced into the material at an angle of 30 to 80 degrees from the perpendicular to the material surface. This angle will vary with the material's thickness. A longitudinal transducer is mounted on plastic wedges cut at specific angles, usually 70, 60, or 45 degrees. By varying the position of the angle beam search unit with respect to the weld, flaws at any location in the weld joint can be detected, as shown in figure 8-10.

(c) Surface waves are generated by mode conversion so that the refracted wave will travel along the surface. Surface waves follow curved surfaces and detect surface and near-surface defects. This technique has many applications in industry, but is seldom used for weld inspection.

b. Equipment. The equipment for ultrasonic weld inspection is a pulse-echo-type ultrasonic test unit that can generate, receive, and present on a CRT screen pulses in the frequency range from 0.2 to 10 megahertz.

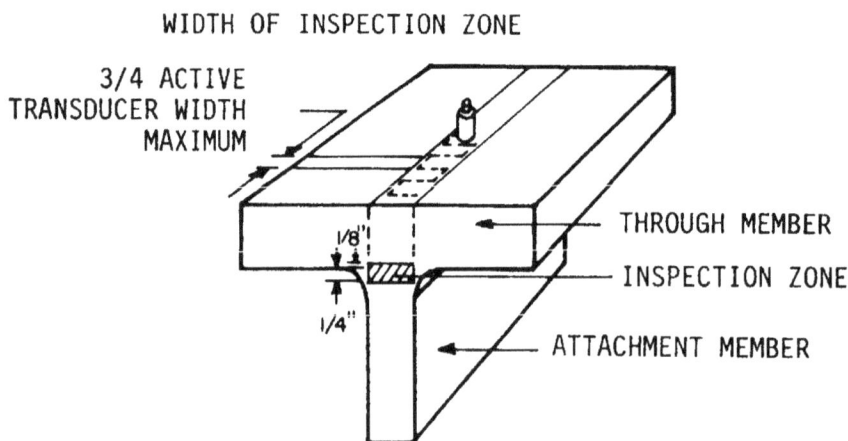

Figure 8-9. Straight beam inspection techniques used in scanning a tee weld

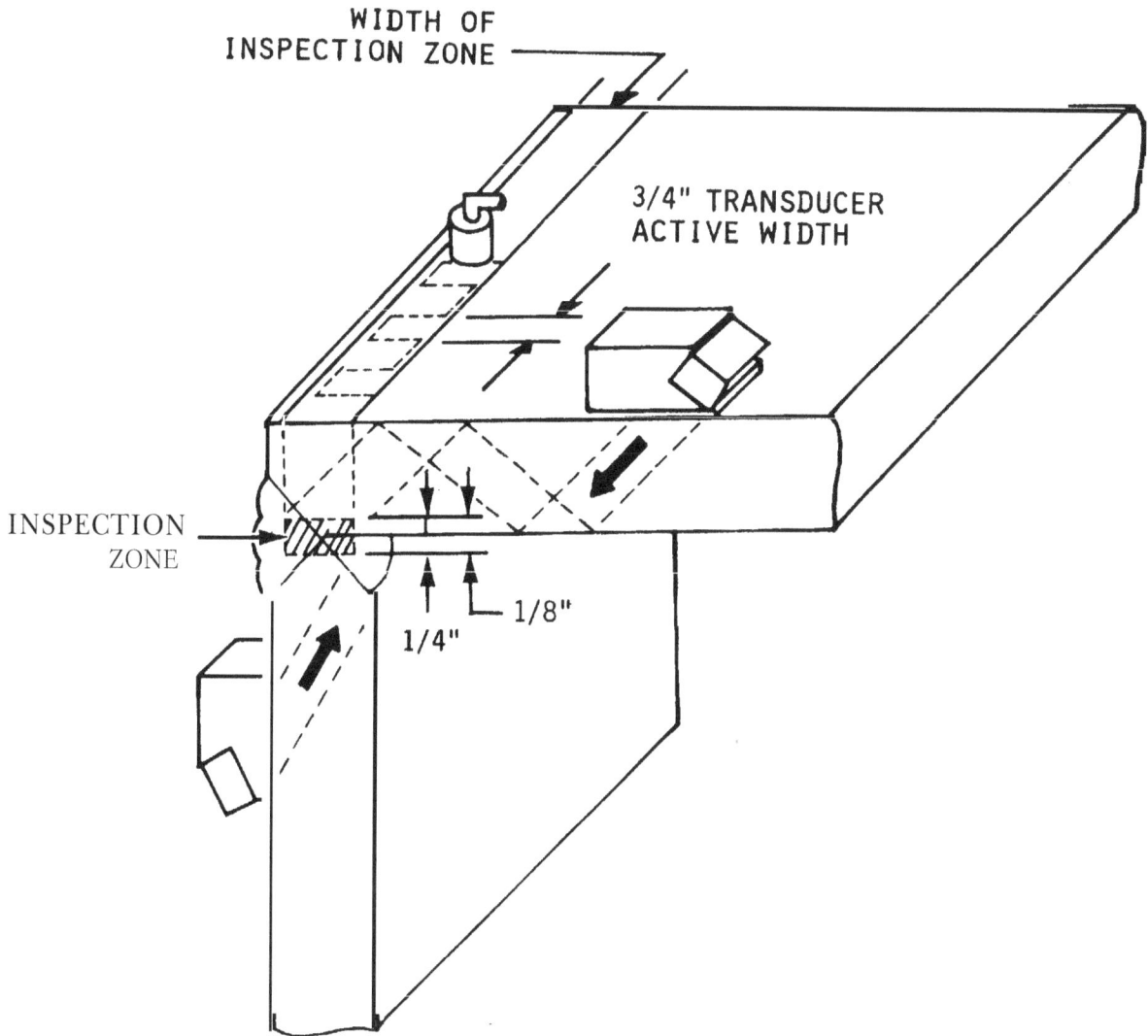

WIDTH OF
INSPECTION ZONE

3/4" TRANSDUCER
ACTIVE WIDTH

INSPECTION
ZONE

1/8"

1/4"

Reprinted from MIL HDBK 333 (USAF), Handbook for Standardization of Nondestructive
Testing Methods, Department of Defense,
1974 (noncopyrighted).

Figure 8-10. Scanning procedure using angle beam and straight beam on a corner weld

(1) Transducers will consist of straight beam and angle beam types in the frequency range of 2 to 2.4 megahertz. Angle beam transducer angles of 70, 60, and 45 degrees are to be used.

(2) A coupling material is needed to exclude air. Typical coupling materials include water, oil, grease, pastes, and glycerine. Generally, the rougher the surface, the more viscous the coupling agent required.

(3) Ultrasonic reference blocks are usually needed to check the sensitivity and performance of ultrasonic instrumentation and transducers for inspecting critical welds. Most standards are manufactured with artificial defects in the form of drilled holes with flat, round, or conical bottoms or slots machined into the surface. AWS D1.1 recommends several standards, the most common being the International Institute of Welding (IIW) reference block shown in figure 8-11.

Inspection procedures. The procedures described conform to ASTM E 164 and AWS D1.1. Ultrasonic inspection procedures are also outlined in appendix U to the ASME Boiler and Pressure Vessel Code, Section VIII, Division 1, and in Section V, Article 5. In ultrasonic inspection, the most important phase is the interpretation of indications. In preparing for an ultrasonic inspection, an operator must consider certain parameters: type and size of transducer, couplant, scanning procedures, peaking techniques, frequency, pulse length, linearity of

indications, distance/time relationship, and sensitivity/time relationship. Other parameters are specimen properties, such as material sound/velocity; specific acoustic impedance; part geometry; material attenuation; and noise level. Each signal peak along the scan line represents a place in time where the acoustic energy has encountered an interface or a multiple of a previously generated signal. By knowing the beam path and spread, the operator can interpret the signal and separate relevant from irrelevant indications. The operator must consider amplitude/distance response and amplitude/area response when determining flaw size. The shape and orientation of the flaw also affect the signal amplitude. In attempting to determine flaw size, an operator must watch both the flaw signal amplitude and the loss of amplitude of the back reflection.

(1) Before any inspection, the ultrasonic unit must be calibrated for sensitivity and horizontal sweep (distance); a calibration block or other recognized method must be used.

(2) The surface of the weld area to be inspected must be free of weld spatter (which will cause rapid wear of the transducer), grease, dirt, oil, and loose scale (which will cause scattering and attenuation). Tight layers of paint need not be removed unless the thickness exceeds 10 roils.

(3) A coupling agent must be used between the search unit and the metal. The base metal is first examined for lamella flaws using a straight beam search unit, and then is inspected using the angle

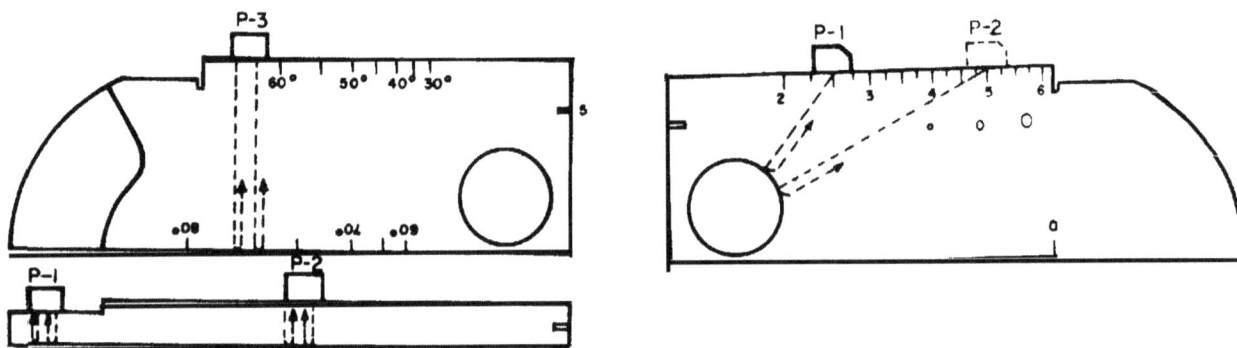

Figure 8-11. Several uses of the IIW block.

3/4 TRANSDUCER
ACTIVE WIDTH

15°

30°

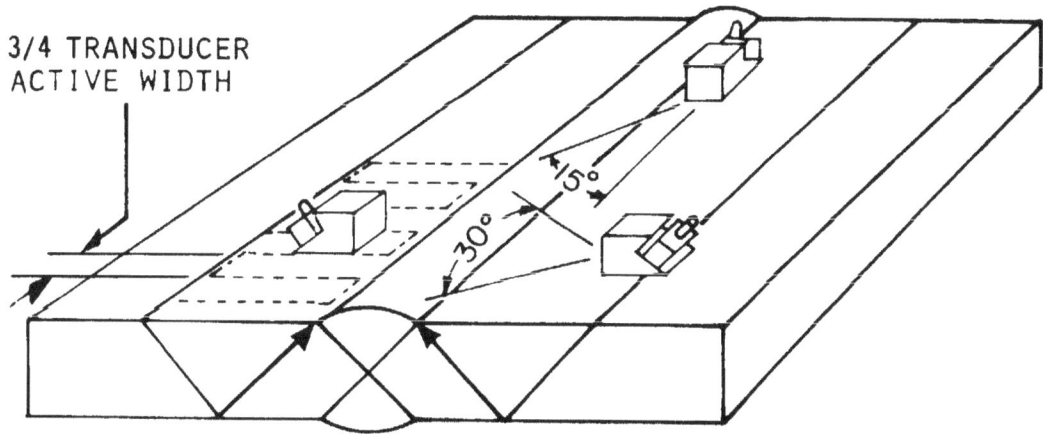

Reprinted from MIL HDBK 333 (USAF), Handbook for Standardization of Nondestructive
Testing Methods, Department of Defense,
1974 (noncopyrighted).

Figure 8-12. Scanning procedures for welds not ground flush.

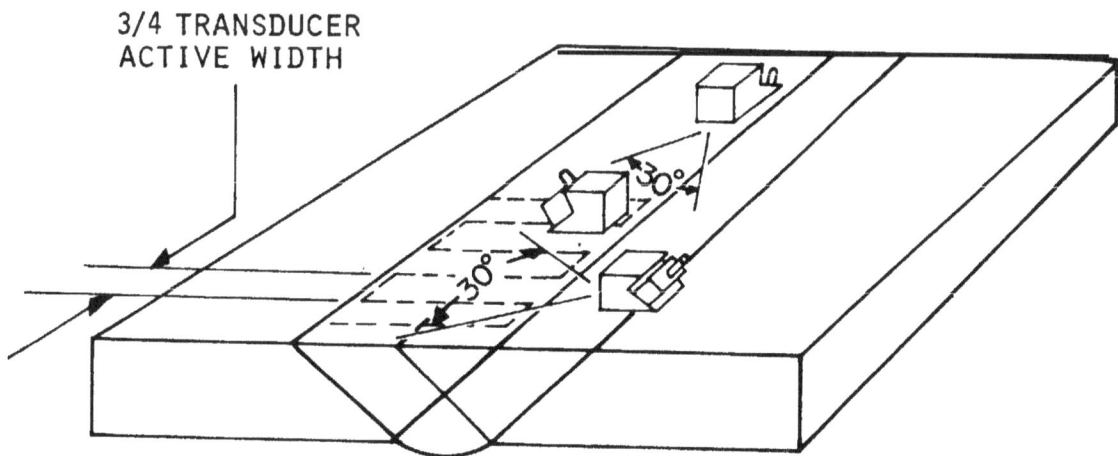

3/4 TRANSDUCER
ACTIVE WIDTH

30°

30°

Reprinted from MIL HDBK 333 (USAF), Handbook for Standardization of Nondestructive
Testing Methods, Department of Defense,
1974 (noncopyrighted).

Figure 8-13. Scanning procedures for welds ground flush.

beam. Where possible, all welds should be scanned from both sides on the beam face for longitudinal and transverse discontinuities. The search unit must be placed on the surface with the sound beam aimed about 90 degrees to the weld and manipulated laterally and longitudinally so that the ultrasonic beam passes through all of the weld metal.

(4) For welds not ground flush (fig 8-12), shear wave is used in four different scans. For longitudinal flaws, sound is directed into the weld from each side. The transducer is oscillated to the left and right with an included angle of about 30 degrees. To detect transverse defects, the transducer is placed on the base metal at the edge of the weld. It is then positioned so that the sound beam makes about a 15-degree angle to the longitudinal axis of the weld. To scan, the search is moved along the weld edge from both sides. For welds ground flush (fig 8-13), scanning is done similarly. However, to detect longitudinal flaws the transducer is moved across the weld. And for transverse defects, the transducer is oscillated left and right through a 30-degree angle while continuously advancing along the top of the weld.

(5) When an indication of a flaw appears on the CRT, the location and position of the transducer are recorded. By using graphs, calculators, or guides, the operator can accurately locate the position of the defect in the weld. By using applicable charts and attenuation factors, the weld discontinuity can be accepted or rejected.

8-10. Destructive testing

In procedure qualification testing and welding development work, metallographic specimens are sometimes removed from a structure to check the quality of the weldment. These tests are used to determine visually the characteristics of the welds. Metallographic test samples are sections cut through the welds in any desired plane, then polished and etched to reveal the structure. These specimens may be examined with the naked eye or with various magnifications, including microscopic, Among the characteristics that can be checked are the soundness, location, and depth of penetration of the welds; the metallurgical structures of the weld, fusion zone, and heat affected zone; the extent and distribution of undesirable inclusions in the weld; hardness gradients; and the number of weld passes. When metallographic specimens are removed from any part of a structure, repairs must be made by qualified welders or welding operators using accepted welding procedures. Peening or heat treatment may be required to develop the full strength of the members cut and to relieve residual stress.

a. Test methods. There are three categories of destructive tests: chemical, hardness, and mechanical tests.

(1) Chemical tests. Chemical tests are generally used to validate the chemical composition or the corrosion resistance of the base and weld metals. Particular compositions of the metals involved, for example, may be examined for conformance to specifications. In addition, chemical analysis of the weld metal can show whether welding produced the expected results, or whether it introduced undesirable constituents into the weld metal. corrosion tests demonstrate a weldment's capability to withstand the corrosive environment to be encountered in service. Because of the cost and time involved, a weldment usually cannot be tested for corrosion resistance by actual use under service conditions. Therefore, accelerated corrosion tests that can be conducted under laboratory conditions have been developed.

(2) Hardness tests. Hardness tests measure the resistance of materials to wear. For most metals, ductility and corrosion resistance decrease as the hardness increases. Since each operation during welding has metallurgical effects, some specifications call for an upper limit to the acceptable hardness of various areas of weld. Hardness testing is done with equipment which, under a specific load, forces a small hardened steel ball or diamond point into the. surface of the metal. The depth of penetration is either measured directly by the machine, or inferred from the dimensions of the impression. By associating a number with each possible impression depth, the inspector can develop a hardness scale. This testing approach is used by the three most common hardness measuring devices: the Brinell, Rockwell, and Vickers hardness testers. Hardness numbers may vary from method to method because of differences in the formulas used to define hardness numbers, in the material type and shape used to make the impression, and in the imposed load. However, tables of approximately equivalent hardness numbers have been constructed.

(3) Mechanical tests. Mechanical tests (exclusive of hardness) have been designed to test several weld properties.

(a) Tensile tests are conducted on specimens machined from a test weld and are used to measure the strength of the weld joint. Specimens are usually taken perpendicular to the weld, which is centered in the specimen (fig 8-14). However, specimens are sometimes taken along the weld and consist entirely of weld metal. Specimens may have round or rectangular cross sections, depending on the requirements of the applicable welding code. The testing machine

WELD

A. RECTANGULAR SPECIMEN

WELD

B. CYLINDRICAL SPECIMEN

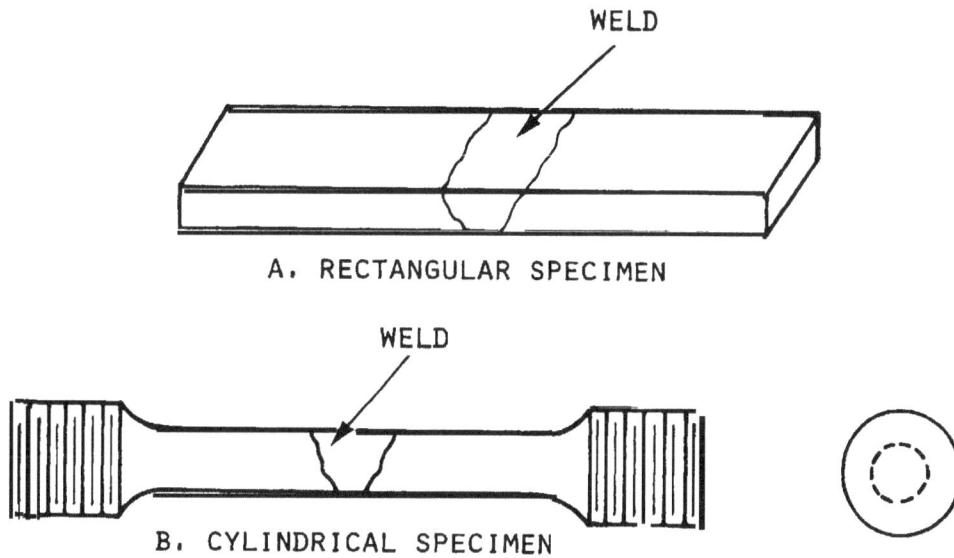

Reprinted from MIL HDBK 58, Thermal Joining of Metals, Processes Other Than Arc
Welding, Department of Defense, 1971 (noncopyrighted).

Figure 8-14. Tensile test specimens.

applies a tensile force until the specimen ruptures. From readings on the machine and measurements of the specimen before and after the test, properties such as yield point or yield strength, ultimate strength, and ductility are calculated. The primary purpose of the test is to demonstrate that the weld metal deposited by the selected procedures meets or exceeds the minimum values specified in the applicable code or specifications.

(b) Guided bend tests indicate a weld's ductility. Test specimens are described as root-bend, face-bend, or side-bend, depending on the surface stretched in bending. Rectangular test specimens similar to those prepared for tensile tests are machined or ground to remove any weld reinforcement. A test jig, such as that shown in figure 8-15, is used to make the bend. with the plunger removed, the specimen is placed across the shoulders of the jig with the weld centered. The plunger is then forced down until the specimen is bent into a U-shape. The elongation of the tension surface is determined by the relationship between the thickness of the specimen and the radius of the die. The

specimen fails if it has cracks or other open defects greater than a specified number and size, or if it fractures.

(c) Free bend tests, also for ductility, use specimens similar to those for guided bend tests. Before the test, gage lines are inscribed across the width of the sample of deposited weld metal. These lines mark off a distance about 1/8 inch less than the width of the weld. The sample is given an initial bend (fig 8-1 6) by supporting the ends or shoulders on rollers, then forcing the center down until the specimen takes a permanent set. Next, a testing machine or device (fig 8-16) is used to compress the sample longitudinally until a crack or depression appears on the convex face of the specimen, or until the specimen is bent double. The load is removed immediately if a defect appears before the specimen is bent double. Percent elongation is calculated from the initial and final distances between the gage marks.

(d) Shear tests of fillet welds are conducted by pulling specimens apart in a testing machine. The dimensions of the specimens make it easy to use the

FORCE

+

PLUNGER
MEMBER

DIE MEMBER

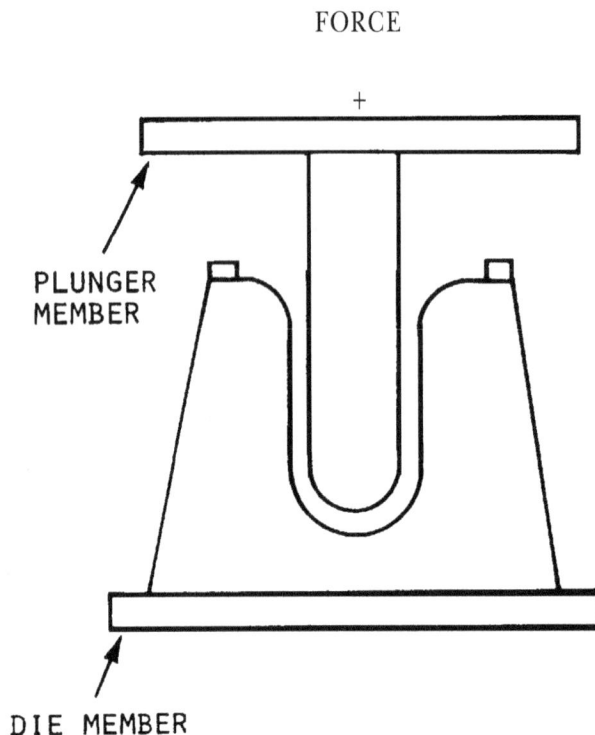

Figure 8-15. Guided bend test jig.

test results to obtain shear strength in pounds per linear inch of weld. Figure 8-17 shows the shear test specimen and indicates where to machine specimens from test weldment.

(e) Nick-break tests are required in some welding codes to detect weld defects. The nick-break test specimens similar to a rectangular tensile-test specimen, except that notches are cut at the center of the weld. The specimen is then broken either by pulling in tension or by bending. The specimen is forced to break in the weld metal because of the notches. After the specimen has been broken, the fracture surfaces are examined for weld-metal defects. If there are more than the minimum allowed, the weld is rejected.

(f) Various types of impact tests are sometimes used to test the fracture toughness of the weld metal when low-alloy, high-strength steels are being welded. These tests measure the weld metal's capability to resist crack propagation under low stress.

b. Sampling technique, Removal of samples by sectioning is an accepted method of weld inspection approved by various pressure-vessel codes. Because the cavity must later be repaired by rewelding, the method is sometimes considered a destructive test. Samples may be taken for chemical analysis, etch tests, subsize tension, or impact tests. The specific method of removing samples depends on the size of specimen needed; hole saws, bolt cutters, cold chisels, or trepanning tools — a special power tool with a hemispherical saw — are often used for sample removal. The samples must be carefully selected to be representative of the weld or base metal being checked.

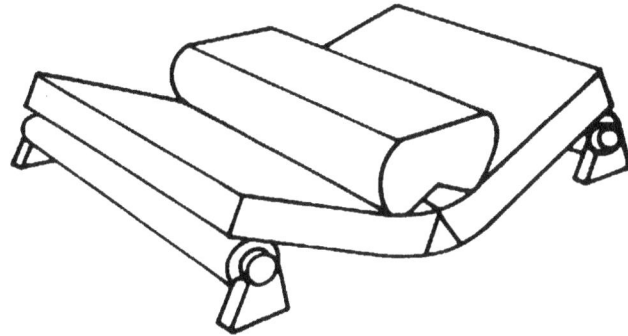

1 INITIAL SET

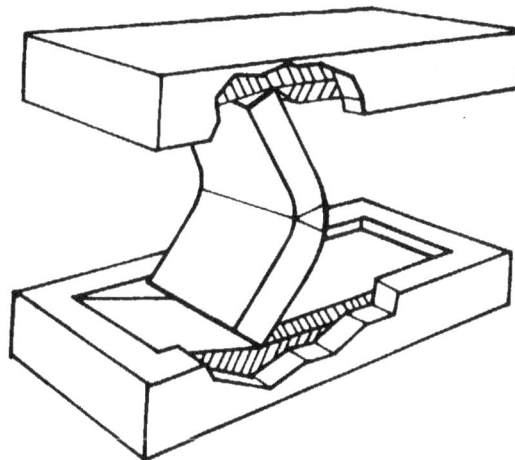

2 COMPRESSION OF SPECIMEN

Reprinted from MIL HDBK 58, Thermal Joining of Metals, Processes Other Than Arc
Welding, Department of Defense, 1971
(noncopyrighted).

Figure 8-16. Free bend test.

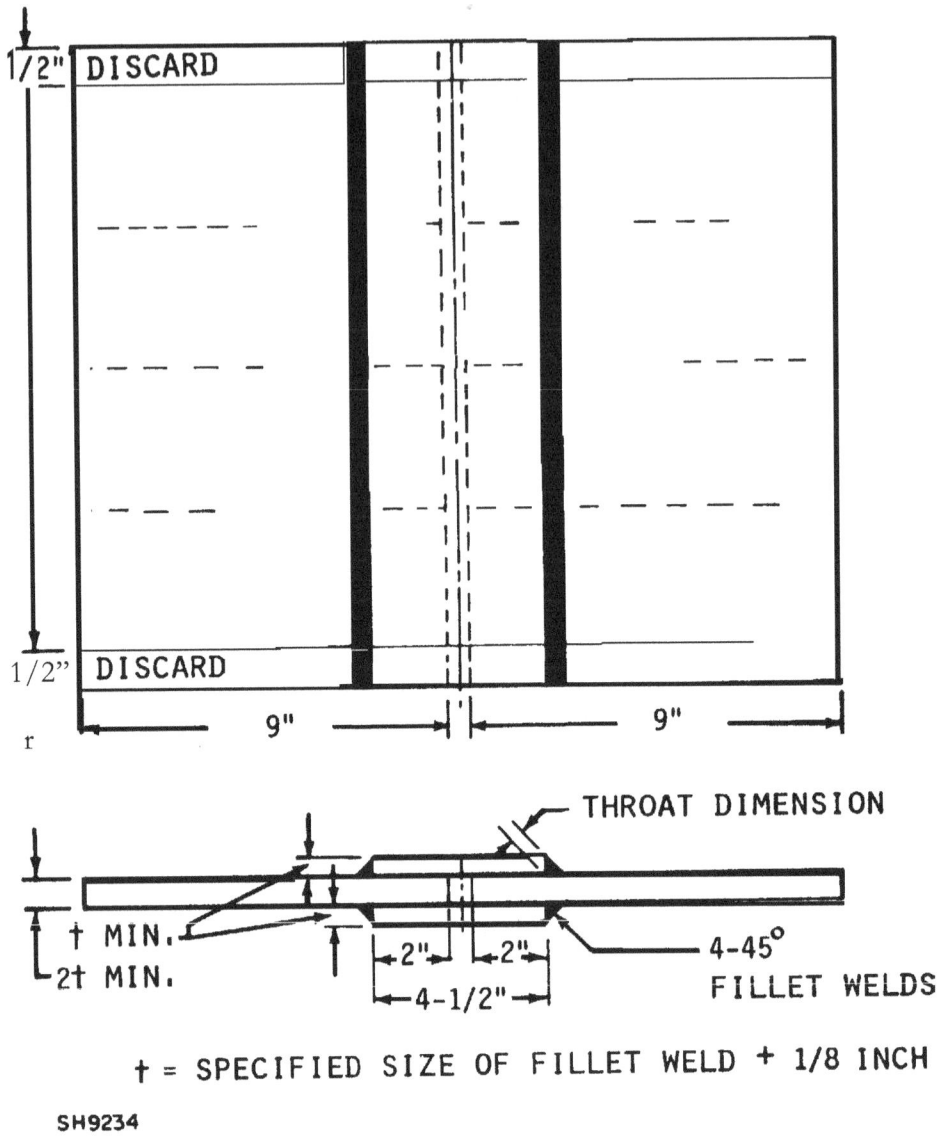

THROAT DIMENSION

t MIN.
2t MIN.

2" 2"
4-1/2"

4-45°
FILLET WELDS

t = SPECIFIED SIZE OF FILLET WELD + 1/8 INCH

SH9234

Reprinted from MIL STD 418C (noncopyrighted).

Figure 8-17. Transverse fillet-weld shear specimen.

8-11. Leak testing

Leak tests are similar to proof tests for closed pressure vessels; the container being tested is filled with a fluid at a specified pressure. The choice of liquid or gas depends on the purpose of the container and the leakage that can be tolerated. For example, containers that are watertight may not be oiltight or gastight. Leaks can be detected in several ways. For oil or water, visual inspection of the outside of the pressure vessel may suffice. Leaking air or gas can be detected by the sound of the escaping gas, by use of a soap film that forms bubbles as gas escapes beneath it, or by immersion in a liquid in which the escaping gas forms bubbles. For hydrostatic or gas tests, a pressure gage attached to the vessel indicates leaks by the drop in pressure after the tests begin. Dyes introduced into liquids and tracers introduced into gases can also indicate leakage. Weld defects that cause leakage are not always detected by the usual nondestructive testing methods. A tight crack or fissure may not appear on a radiograph, yet will form a leak path. A production operation, such as forming or a proof test, may make leaks develop in an otherwise acceptable weld joint. A leak test is usually done on the completed vessel if all of the weld joints can be inspected; at this stage there will be no more fabricating operations after the inspection. Inspection is easier if the vessel is empty, The most common types of leak testing are discussed below.

a. The pressure-rise test method is used to see whether any leaks exist. In this test, the part being inspected is attached to a vacuum pump and evacuated to a pressure of ().5 psi absolute. when this pressure is reached, the connections to the vacuum pump are sealed off, and the internal pressure of the part is measured immediately. The pressure is measured again after at least 5 minutes (with the item still sealed off from the vacuum pump). If the pressure in the evacuated space remains essentially constant, the welds are free of leaks. If there is a pressure rise, at least one leak is present, and the helium-leak test described in b below must be used,

b. The helium-leak test is more precise than the pressure-rise method and is used to find the exact location of these leaks. Helium-leak testing is slow, however, so it normally is not used to inspect large items unless a leak definitely exists. This inspection method requires the use of a helium mass spectrometer to detect the presence of helium gas. The mass spectrometer is connected to the pumping system between the vacuum pump and the item being inspected. Then the item is evacuated by a vacuum pump to a pressure of less than 50 microns of mercury. The mass spectrometer can detect helium in the evacuated space. A small jet of helium gas is directed at the side of the weld joint exposed to the atmosphere. If there is a leak, some of the helium is sucked through it into the evacuated space, and the mass spectrometer immediately indicates the presence of helium. Of course, if no leak is present, no helium will enter the evacuated space and no indication will appear on the mass spectrometer. To determine the exact location of leaks, the jet of helium is moved along the surface of the weld joint. At the same time, an inspector carefully watches the mass spectrometer. If there is an indication, the leak is at the point where the helium jet is hitting the surface of the weld joint.

c. To detect leaks, the ultrasonic translator detector uses the ultrasonic sounds of gas molecules escaping from a vessel under pressure or vacuum. The sound created is in the frequency range of 35,000 and 45,000 Hertz, which is above the range of human hearing and is therefore classified as ultrasonic. Certain characteristics of these frequencies are useful for detections. They are outside the range of most plant and machine noise, and the short wave length of these frequencies permits the use of highly directional microphones. Any system or vessel that can be pressurized or evacuated to a pressure of 3 psi can be inspected. The operator simply listens to the translated ultrasonic sounds while moving a hand-held probe along the weld (in the same way that a flashlight. is used to illuminate the suspected leak locations). The detectors are simple to operate and require minimum operator training.

d. Some of the following tests — particularly the air-soap solution test — can be conducted on a vessel during or after assembly. The inspector can locate large defects in order to reduce the time needed for final leak testing. After testing, vessels should be thoroughly cleaned to remove all traces of soap solution.

(1) Hydrostatic test. This test should conform to the applicable requirements of a particular vessel or system. only distilled or deionized (demineralized) water having a pH of 6 to 8 and an impurity content not greater than 5 ppm is used. Traces of water should be removed from the inside before final leak testing is begun.

(2) Water submersion test. In this test, the vessel is completely submerged in clean water. The interior is pressurized with gas, but the design pressure must not be exceeded. The size and number of any gas bubbles indicates the size of leaks,

(3) Soap solution test, In this test, the vessel is subjected to an internal gas pressure not exceeding the design pressure. A soap or equivalent solution is

applied so that connections and welded joints can be examined for leaks.

(4) Air-ammonia test. This test involves introducing air into the vessel until so percent of the design pressure is needed. Anhydrous ammonia is then introduced into the vessel until 55 percent of the design pressure is reached; air is then reintroduced until the design pressure is reached. Each joint is carefully examined by using as a probe either a swab wetted with 10N solution of muriatic acid (HCL), a sulphur candle, or sulphur dioxide. A wisp of white smoke indicates a leak.

(5) Halide torch test. In this test, the vessel is pressurized to a value not exceeding the design pressure; a mixture of S O percent Freon and carbon dioxide or 50 percent Freon and nitrogen is used.

Each joint is carefully probed with a halide torch to detect leaks, which are indicated by a change in the color of the flame.

(6) Halogen snifter test. A Freon inert gas mixture is introduced into the vessel until the design pressure is reached. About 1 ounce of Freon for every 30 cubic feet of vessel volume is required. The inspector passes the probe of a halogen vapor analyzer over the area to be explored. This probe is held about 1/2 inch from the surface being tested and is moved at about 1/2 inch per second. Since the instrument is responsive to cigarette smoke and vapor from newly dry-cleaned clothing, the air should be kept clean where the test is being done. In addition, the test should be done in a substantially draft-free enclosure.

CHAPTER 9

SAFETY

9-1. General

The safety of the welding operators, foreman, and inspectors at the construction job site is a primary consideration. All precautions must be taken to ensure the safe completion of the construction project. The Occupational Safety and Health Administration (OSHA) of the U.S. Department of Labor has issued Health and Safety Standards covering such topics as radiation protection, welding, cutting and heating, use of ladders and scaffolds, steel erection, and hearing and head protection. Most of the standards for welding are in Code of Federal Regulations, Title 29, Chapter XVII, Part 1910.

9-2. Hazards

a. Welding and cutting. When welding and cutting is being done, three major safety hazards must be considered and adequate precautions taken. First, the eyes and exposed skin must be protected from the intense light radiation and the heat of the welding arc and flames. Second, welding, cutting, and grinding operations must be prevented from causing fires. Third, care must be taken in handling, welding, and cutting containers that have held combustible or toxic materials. Cutting or welding also must be done carefully if materials in the fluxes, coatings, and base metals produce explosive or toxic fumes when heated. There are other safety considerations for welding and cutting operations; all personnel involved should be familiar with the requirements of the OSHA safety standards. The AWS also publishes and distributes information on safe welding and cutting practices.

b. Radiographic inspection. Radiographic inspection involves ionizing radiation. Individuals can be protected from this radiation primarily by shielding and distance. For information on safe procedures and practices for radiography, refer to Title 10, Code of Federal Regulations; the American Society for Non-Destructive Testing; and AWS.

c. Noise levels. Hearing loss, either partial or total, is a direct result of working without proper ear protection at steel construction sites. Contractors must conform to OSHA standards for permissible noise levels and time durations.

d. Air quality. Welding and cutting operations increase dust and ozone levels near the construction. Welding galvanized steel also releases zinc oxide, which can be very hazardous to welding operators and their assistants. Therefore, proper ventilation should be provided for all personnel at the welding site. Particular attention should be paid to safety when personnel are welding inside large tanks. There should always be ventilation for such an operation.

APPENDIX A

REFERENCES

Government Publications

Department of Defense.

MIL-C-15726E	Copper-Nickel Alloy, Rod, Flat Products (Flat Wire, Strip, Sheet, Bar and Plate), and Forgings.
MIL-E-22200F	General Specification for Electrodes, Welding Covers.
MIL-E-18193	Electrode, Welding, Carbon Steel and Alloy Steel, Bare, Coiled.
MIL-E-19822A	Electrodes, Welding, Bare, High-Yield Steel.
MIL-E-23765/1D	Electrodes and Rods-Welding, Bare, Solid, Mild and Alloy Steel.
MIL-E-23765/2B	Electrode and Rod-Welding, Bare, Solid, Low Alloy Steel.
MIL-I-6868	Inspection Process, Magnetic Particle.
MIL-R-11468	Radiographic Inspection, Soundness Requirements for Arc and Gas Welds in Steel,
MIL-R-11470	Radiographic Inspection, Qualification of Equipment, Operators and Procedures.
MIL-R-45774(2)	Radiographic Inspection, Soundness Requirements for Fusion Welds in Aluminum and Magnesium Missile Components.
MIL-STD-00453B	Radiographic Inspection.
MIL-STD-271E	Nondestructive Testing Requirement for Metals.
MIL-STD-410D	Nondestructive Testing Personnel Qualification and Certification (Eddy Current, Liquid Penetrant, Magnetic Particle, Radiographic and Ultrasonic).
MIL-STD-779	Reference Radiographic for Steel Fusion Welds, Vol. I, Vol. II, Vol. III.

Department of the Army.

TM 9-237	Welding Theory and Application.

Nuclear Regulatory Commission.
1717 H St., NW, Washington, D.C. 20555

Genera l Service s Administration (GSA).
18th and F Streets, NW, Washington, D.C. 20405 Code of Federal Regulations, Title 10, Chapter I, Parts 20 and 34, and Title 29, Chapter XVII, Part 1910, published by the Office of the Federal Register, National Archives and Records Service (Updated Annually)

Occupational Safety and Health Administration (OSHA),
Bureau of National Affairs, 1231 25th St., NW, Washington, D.C. 20037

Nongovernment Publications

Aerospace Materials Specification (AMS), Society of Automotive Engineers, 400 Commonwealth Drive, Warrendale, PA 15096

AMS 2635B	Radiographic Inspection (updated periodically).
AMS 2640H	Magnetic Particle Inspection (updated periodically).
AMS 2645G	Fluorescent Penetrant Inspection (updated periodically).
AMS 2646B	Contrast Dye Penetrant Inspection (updated periodically).

American Institute of Steel Construction (AISC), 400 N. Michigan Ave., 8th Floor, Chicago, IL 60611
Manual of Steel Construction

Aluminum Association, inc. (AA), 818 Connecticut Avenue, NW Washington, DC 20006

American Concrete Institute (ACI), P.O. Box 19150, Detroit, MI 48219

ACI 318-77	Building Code Requirements for Reinforced Concrete.

American Iron and Steel Institute (AISI), 1000 16th Street, NW, Washington, DC 20036
Industry Practices for Ultrasonic Nondestructive Testing of Steel Tubular Products.
Ultrasonic Inspection of Steel Products.

American National Standards institute (ANSI,, 1430 Broadway, New York, NY 10018

ANSI B31.1-80	Power Piping.

American Petroleum Institute (API), 1801 K Street, Washington, DC 20006
API-STD-1104   API Specification for Field Welding of Pipelines.
American Society for Metals (ASM), Metals park, OH 44073
     Metals Handbook, ASM Handbook Committee, Volume 6: Welding and Brazing (9th Ed., 1983).
American Society for Nondestructive Testing (ASNT), 3200 Riverside Drive, Columbus, OH 43221
ASNT-TC-lA   Recommended Practice Nondestructive Testing Personnel Qualification and Certification (updated periodically).
     Nondestructive Testing Handbook, Vols. I and II, Robert McMaster, cd., The Ronald Press Co.
American Society for Testing and Materials (ASTM), 1916 Race Street, Philadelphia, PA 19103
ASTM A514-82   Specification for High-Yield Strength, Quenched and-Tempered Alloy Steel Plate, Suitable for Welding. (Rev. A)
ASTM A517/ A517M-82   Specification for Pressure Vessel Alloy Steel, High-Strength, Quenched and Tempered.
ASTM A36-81   Specification for Structural Steel. (Rev. A)
ASTM A242-81   Specification for High-Strength Low-Alloy Structural Steel.
ASTM A441-81   Specification for High-Strength Low-Alloy Structural Manganese Vanadium Steel.
ASTM A572-82   Specification for High-Strength Low-Alloy Columbium-Vanadium Steels of Structural Quality.
ASTM A53-82   Specification for Pipe, Steel, Black and Hot-Dipped Zinc-Coated Welded and Seamless.
ASTM A106-82   Specification for Seamless Carbon Steel Pipe for High-Temperature Service.
ASTM A139-74   Specification for Electric-Fusion (Arc) -Welded Steel Pipe (Sizes 4 in. and over) (R 1980).
ASTM A691-81   Specification for Carbon and Alloy Steel Pipe, Electric-Fusion-Welded for High-Pressure Services at High Temperatures.
ASTM A203-81   Specification for Pressure Vessel Plates Alloy Steel, Nickel.
ASTM A588-81   Specification for High-Strength Low-Alloy Structural Steel with 50,000 psi Minimum Yield Point to 4 in. Thick.
ASTM A134-80   Specification for Pipe, Steel, Electric-Fusion (Arc) -Welded (Sizes NPS16 and over).
ASTM A671-80   Specification for Electric-Fusion-Welded Steel Pipe for Atmospheric and Lower Temperatures.
ASTM A672-81   Specification for Electric-Fusion-Welded Steel Pipe for High-Pressure Service at Moderate Temperatures.
ASTM A710-79   Specification for Low Carbon Age-Hardening Nickel-Copper-Chromium-Molybdenum-Columbium and Nickel-Copper-Columbium Alloy Steels.
ASTM E390-75   Radiographs for Steel Fusion Welds.
ASTM E709-80   Practice for Magnetic Particle Examination.
ASTM E94-77   Radiographic Testing, Standard for Recommended Practice.
ASTM E138-81   Standard Method for Wet Magnetic Particle Inspection.
ASTM E142-77   Standard Method for Controlling Quality of Radiographic Testing.
ASTM E164-81   Standard Recommended Practice for Ultrasonic Contact Examination of Weldments.
ASTM E165-80   Standard Recommended Practice for Liquid Penetrant Inspection Method.
American Society of Mechanical Engineers (ASME), United Engineering Center, 345 East Forty-Seventh Street, New York, NY 10017
     Boiler and Pressure Vessel Code (1974). Section II, Material Specification. Section III, Nuclear Power Plant Components.
     Section V, Nondestructive Examination. Section VIII, Pressure Vessels. Section IX, Welding Qualification.
American Welding Society (AWS), P.O. Box 351040, 550 LeJeune Road, Miami, FL 33135
AWS A3.0-80   Welding Terms and Definitions Including Terms for Brazing, Soldering, Thermal Spraying, and Thermal Cutting.
AWS A5.1-81   Specifications for Carbon Steel Covered Arc Welding Electrodes.

AWS A5.4-81	Specification for Corrosion-Resisting Chromium and Chromium-Nickel Steel Covered Electrodes.
AWS A5.5-81	Specification for Low-Alloy Steel Covered Arc-Welding Electrodes.
AWS A5.9-81	Specification for Corrosion-Resisting and Chromium-Nickel Steel Bare and Composite Metal Cored and Stranded Arc Welding Electrodes and Welding Rods.
AWS A5.14-76	Specification for Nickel and Nickel Alloy Bare Welding Rods and Electrodes.
AWS A5.17-80	Specification for Bare Carbon Steel Electrodes and Fluxes for Submerged Arc Welding.
AWS A5.18-79	Specification for Carbon Steel Filler Metals Gas Shielded Arc Welding.
AWS A5.20-79	Specification for Carbon Steel Electrodes for Flux Cored Arc Welding.
AWS A5.22-80	Specification for Flux-Cored Corrosion-Resisting Chromium and Chromium-Nickel Steel Electrodes.
AWS A5.23-80	Specification for Bare Low-Alloy Steel Electrodes and Fluxes for Submerged Arc Welding.
AWS D1.1-83	Structural Welding Code—Steel.
AWS A5.11-76	Specifications for Nickel and Nickel Alloy Covered Welding Electrodes.
AWS A5.10-80	Specification for Aluminum and Aluminum Alloy Bare Welding Rods and Electrodes.
AWS D12.1-75	Reinforcing Steel Welding Codes. (superseded by AWS D1.4-79)
AWS D19.0-72	Welding Zinc-Coated Material (superseded by AWS C2.2)
American Welding Society (AWS),	P. O. Box 351040,550 LeJeune Road, Miami, FL 33135
	Welding Handbook
	Volume 1, Fundamentals of Welding, 6th Edition (1968)
	Volume 2, Welding Processes, 7th Edition (1978)
	Volume 3, Welding Processes, 7th Edition (1980)
	Volume 4, Metals and Their Weldability, 6th Edition (1968)
	Volume 5, Application of Welding, 6th Edition (1968)
Welding Research Council,	345 E. 47th Street, New York, NY 10017
	Weldability of Steels, Robert D. Stout and W. D'Orville Doty, 1971

APPENDIX B

QUALIFICATION TESTING

B-1. General

A project manager must determine the ability of a manufacturer, contractor, fabricator, or erector to produce quality welds consistently. Qualification requirements insure that properly trained welding personnel use approved procedures and adequate equipment. The qualification requirement includes a wide range of materials, procedures, processes, equipment, and personnel. For a construction project, a weld quality assurance program uses qualification testing for the welding procedure and the welding personnel.

B-2. Procedure qualification

a. Purpose. The purpose of the procedure qualification test is to demonstrate that certain procedures produce welds of suitable mechanical properties and soundness.

b. Method. Small test plates with the same chemical composition as the production weldments are welded with the proposed production procedure. The joint geometry, welding process, welding parameters, filler metals, shielding materials, and welding position used to make the test plates are also the same as or equivalent to those for the actual production weldment. The plates are then tested to see whether the weld's soundness and mechanical properties meet the acceptance standards of the production weld. The requirements for qualifying a welding procedure are governed by the codes concerning the weld's specific application.

c. Testing.

(1) The procedure qualification plates are usually tested nondestructively, with the same tests required for the production weld. The plate must meet the nondestructive test acceptance standards of the code applicable to the weld's specified use,

(2) Tensile and bend tests are normally used for procedure qualification plates. Some welds also require the nick-break test, impact tests, and metallographic examination.

(3) Tensile test specimens are removed so that the long axis of the specimen is transverse to the welding direction and is centered on the weld's centerline. The actual specimen geometry varies widely to meet requirements of various welding codes. The specimens may be round or flat and may have a reduced section; the flat specimen may have the weld reinforcement removed. To be acceptable, the tensile specimens must exceed the minimum requirements in the welding code for the type of material being used. The primary purpose of the tensile test is to demonstrate that the weld metal deposited by the selected procedure is strong enough to meet the design requirements.

(4) Three types of bend tests are used for procedure qualification. Root-bend and face-bend tests are used on materials up to 3/8-inch thick. Side-bend tests are used for thicker materials. The names of these procedures refer to the surface that is stretched in tension during bending. In the root-bend test, the root of the weld is placed in tension. In the face-bend and side-bend tests, the weld crown and a transverse cross section, respectively, are put in tension during bending. The specimens are machined or ground to remove the weld reinforcement and then bent around a die of specified radius. The amount of elongation of the tension surface is usually about 20 percent. The bend test indicates the ductility of the weld metal and detects the small defects in the weld that tend to open up and become readily visible. The acceptance criterion for bend tests is that no fissures exceeding a specified length (usually 1/8 inch) be present on the tension surface after bending.

(5) Some welding codes require nick-break tests to detect weld defects. The nick-break test specimen is similar to a rectangular tensile-test specimen, except that notches are cut at the center of the weld. The specimen is then broken either by pulling it in tension or by bending it. The notches cause the specimen to break in the weld metal. After this, the fracture surfaces are examined for weld metal defects. If there are too many defects, the weld is rejected.

(6) Various types of impact tests are sometimes used to test the fracture toughness of the weld metal when low-alloy, high-strength steels are being welded. These tests are designed to measure the capability of the weld metal to resist crack propagation under low-stress conditions.

(7) Metallographic examination involves polishing, etching, and examining weld sections under low magnification to detect porosity, cracks, or other defects in the weld metal. This test maybe required for certain applications, particularly when the weld

configuration does not allow meaningful test results to be obtained by the mechanical property test methods discussed above.

d. Usefulness of procedure qualification. The procedure qualification test is useful for demonstrating the quality and properties of the weld before its production. Since it is almost impossible to duplicate actual production welding conditions, this test is conducted under simulated conditions. In an actual welding situation, conditions arise that could not have been anticipated when the procedure was being qualified (e.g., abrupt weather changes). Therefore, the production phase must be closely supervised so that such conditions are noticed as they occur. If these factors can alter the quality of the weld, they should be evaluated.

B-3. Welder and welding operator qualification

a. General. Weld quality is determined by the specific welding procedure and by the ability of the welder or welding operator to apply that procedure. Welder qualification tests determine the operator's ability to produce sound welds that conform to the procedure specification. The tests indicate whether the welder or welding operator can produce acceptable welds, but do not indicate whether he/she will produce acceptable welds during actual production. Consequently, during the construction process, the welds must be inspected before and after completion.

b. Method. In personnel qualification testing, the welder or welding operator is required to weld a small test plate in a material which is the same as or similar to that of the actual production weldment. The qualified procedure for that weldment must be used. The qualification plate is then nondestructively examined and destructively tested. These steps insure that the weld soundness meets the minimum acceptance standards of the welding code governing the particular application.

c. Testing. Testing methods used for personnel qualification tests usually include the nondestructive examinations applicable to the specific job and any combination of the bend tests described previously. In some instances, nick-break tests may also be required because they examine weld soundness rather than weld metal properties. Tensile tests are usually not required for examining personnel qualifications.

d. Usefulness of personnel qualifications. The personnel qualification tests assure a customer that the welders have been screened and are capable of producing welds that conform to procedure and specification requirements. These tests do not guarantee that the welder will produce satisfactory welds each time, but do tend to eliminate welders whose work is never acceptable. As with procedure qualifications, the value of personnel qualifications increases when the production welding conditions are simulated as closely as possible.

BIBLIOGRAPHY

A. Departments of the Army and the Air Force Publications:

ATAC-STD-113, Reference Standards and Radiographic Procedures for Partial Penetration Aluminum Welds. U.S. Army Tank Automotive Command (ATAC), Warren, MI (1969).

ATAC-STD-114, Reference Standards and Radiographic Procedures for Partial Penetration Steel Welds. USATAC, Warren, MI (1969).

MIL-HDBK-55, Radiography Nondestructive Testing Series. Department of Defense (DOD), Washington, DC (1 April 1966).

MIL-HDBK-56, Materials and Material Processes Series Arc Welding. DOD, Washington, DC (1 July 1968).

MIL-HDBK-58, Thermal Joining of Metals, Processes Other Than Arc Welding. DOD, Washington, DC (1 August 1971).

MIL-HDBK-333 (USAF), Handbook for Standardization of Nondestructive Testing Methods, Vol. I and Vol. II. DOD, Washington, DC (10 April 1974).

MIL-HDBK-723A, Steel and Iron Wrought Products. DOD, Washington, DC (30 November 1970).

MIL-STD-418C, Mechanical Test for Welded Joints (Use ANSI/AWS B4.0, Methods for Mechanical Testing of Welds). American Welding Society (AWS), Miami, FL (1977).

TM 5-805-7, Welding: Design Procedures and Inspection. Department of the Army, Washington, DC (15 March 1968).

Weber, R. A., Weldability Characteristics of Construction Steels A36, A514, and A516. U.S. Army Construction Engineering Research Laboratory (CERL), Champaign, IL. Technical Report M-302/ADA111886 (1981).

B. Publications of Associations:

AMS-2630A, Ultrasonic Testing. Society of Automotive Engineers (SAE), Warrendale, PA (updated periodically).

AMS-2635C, Radiographic Testing, SAE, Warrendale, PA (updated periodically).

AMS-2640H, Magnetic Particle Inspection. SAE, Warrendale, PA (updated periodically).

AMS-2645G, Fluorescent Penetrant Inspection. SAE, Warrendale, PA (updated periodically).

AMS-3646B, Contrast Dye Penetrant Inspection. SAE, Warrendale, PA (updated periodically).

AMS-3155B, Oil, Fluorescent Penetrant, Water Soluble (updated periodically).

AMS-3156B, Oil, Fluorescent Penetrant, Water Soluble (updated periodically).

ANSI B31.8, Gas Transmission and Distribution Piping Systems. American National Standards Institute (ANSI), New York, NY (1982).

CMN, Guide to the Welding and Weldability of C-MN Steels and C-MN Micro-Alloyed Steels, IIW, Miami, FL (available from AWS) (1980).

CS, Recommendations for Arc Welded Joints in Clad Steel Construction, IIW, American Council, Miami, FL (available from AWS) (1976).

FF, Fatigue Fractures in Welded Construction, IIW, American Council, Miami, FL (available from AWS) (1972).

HR, Handbook of Arc Welded Joints in Clad Steel Construction, IIW, American Council, Miami, FL (available from AWS) (1975).

RD, Radiographs of Welds, IIW, American Council, Miami, FL (available from AWS) (1975).

RRS, Steel, International Institute of Welding (IIW), American Council, Miami, FL (available from AWS) (1975).

UTL, Ultrasonic Testing in 11 Languages, IIW, American Council, Miami, FL (available from AWS) (1974).

Welding Inspection, AWS Committee on Methods of Inspection, AWS, Miama, FL (1968).

Welding Metallurgy, Carbon and Alloy Steels, Vols. 1 and 2 (George Linnert), 3rd edition. American Welding Society (AWS), Miami, FL (1965).

By Order of the Secretary of the Army:

JOHN A. WICKHAM, JR.
General, United States Army
Chief of Staff

Official:

DONALD J. DELANDRO
Brigadier General, United States Army
The Adjutant General

Distribution:
Army: To be distributed in accordance with DA Form 12-34B, requirements for TM 5-800 Series: Engineering and Design for Real Property Facilities.

☆ U.S. GOVERNMENT PRINTING OFFICE: 1985—480-255

www.ingramcontent.com/pod-product-compliance
Lightning Source LLC
Chambersburg PA
CBHW081659270326
41933CB00017B/3222